Be Coming Me
"Back to Basics"
by

Claire Rayner

Cover Design by : Frederick Isaacs
ISBN: 978-0-620-82526-9

OUR DEEPEST FEAR

Our deepest fear is not that we are inadequate.
Our deepest fear is that we are powerful beyond measure.

It is our light that most frightens us.
We ask ourselves, "Who am I to be brilliant, gorgeous, talented,
and fabulous"?

Actually, who are you not to be?
You are a child of God.

Your playing small does not serve the world.
As we are liberated from our own fear, our presence automatically
liberates others.

Marianne Williamson

Aimee,
This is for you.

May the longtime sun Shine upon you, all Love surround you, and
the pure Light within you, guide your way home.

Traditional Sufi Blessing

DEDICATED TO MOM AND DAD

Through you learned the value of living a life of impeccability. Thank you for your never ending and consistent love, support and guidance. I'm so grateful.

CONTENTS

INTRODUCTION

The concept for the book came about early in 2002 whilst traveling to Uganda and Tanzania. At the time had been employed in the Advertising Industry for 14 years as a Radio Producer and on that trip was working for Saatchi & Saatchi Advertising Agency as their Africa Radio Producer working extensively for Guinness Africa handling all their Music and Radio productions.

Having been blessed with being able to afford a couple of trips abroad, and through work, got to experience Africa as well. Through my travels, it was quite apparent how much pain and suffering was going on. No matter where you were in the world, it was everywhere.

Couldn't help but notice how big the gap was between the "rich" and the "poor". Why was that? Was it because the "wealthy" knew something those who were "poor" didn't?

Becoming consciously aware really opened my eyes to my surroundings, was beginning to see things in a whole new light bringing about a change in my perspective. Having completed a John Kehoe Mind Power course 2 years prior, led me to believe that if we could educate our young ones by teaching them the "rules of life", we could empower them at a young age.

Imagine knowing where you are going and what you are going to do, and have the confidence and passion to do just that, by the time you graduate from college?

Starting with going "Back to Basics", the Value system, combined with Metaphysics and Mind Power techniques, can not only teach and empower you, but also enrich and strengthen your Spiritual and Religious belief systems, whilst at the same time facilitate Religious and Spiritual growth. This, in turn, will increase your faith as well as benefit you by helping you find you inner strength and in return gain confidence, raising your self-esteem and sense of self.

Our Value System taught to some of us as children, taken so for granted, sometimes forgotten. The simple life skills acquired through our Spiritual Leaders, parents, family, and friends. "The Ten Commandments". If fortunate enough to know them, and can live by them, can completely change your reality.

Why should only those who are fortunate have access to these simple "Rules of Life"? It is believed when children are brought up in underlying conditions it affects their rate of development and these effects could be felt globally.

Everyone should have access to the information as they form the foundations of your life and the success of it.

We are one. Share the Knowledge. Every thought or action sends a ripple that affects everyone.

If only everyone knew you have access to the Power to give yourself what you want. It all lies within you.

You have the Power.
You are the Power.
If you can dream it, you can have it.

Driving through the streets of Mexico City it suddenly hit me. This is it; I was going to do what I could do, to use the knowledge, facilities, and expertise gained in my career to get the "learning's/messages" across. This is what I am meant to do. Realizing then, that my whole life and time spent in the Advertising world was forming the basis of doing something so much more fulfilling, and in return will give my life so much more meaning. I loved my job and loved what I was doing yet always felt this emptiness. Was always looking for something to fill that void, didn't know what it was, has always been with me, and never been able to shake it. Something was always missing.

The thought of this got me buzzing. I knew how much I wanted to do this, so set off home brimming with excitement and joy at the prospect of getting these messages across. Finally, I had found something I could get excited about, something that would "give" to others and help make a difference. It gave me a sense of purpose. And the void simply disappeared.

It was time to share the knowledge. Teach, get the messages to, and empower all.

And so in June 2002, the journey began. Whilst holding my day job, my spare hours were spent brainstorming, conceptualizing, developing a team and searching for funding.

The concept was presented to many blue-chip clients over a period of 8 years who showed a lot of interest, yet any attempts at funding were not showing any sign of success. Having limited time available made the process and movement painstakingly slow. Was finding it all very exhausting, frustrating, disappointing and the rejections were getting to me. As easy as it would have been to just give up on it I couldn't. Knew I would never be happy unless I kept on going and did the work. This was a crazy dream, however, wasn't ready to give up on it.

From the time I committed to the project, I never realized I had found my Purpose. The journey began when I took action. The commitment set in doing the work required to embrace and practice it. No matter how long it takes, it will be well worth it.

Almost immediately my personal life seemed to do an about turn. There were many twists and turns, challenges and painful moments, yet at the same time life was truly very exciting, my beautiful daughter was born in 2004, and I was growing a lot.

Life became very full. I was happy and loving being a mom. Maintained my Advertising career whilst at the same time gave attention and action to my passion project. Then 2009 rolled in and proved to be the most traumatic time for us. By now I'd been a self-employed contractor to the Ad Industry for 8 years, and within a three month period my mom passed away suddenly, I lost my home of 8 years, and my career took a tumble as the recession first started showing itself. News of budget cuts quickly filtered in at work, so things were not looking good at all. My income was badly affected and with everything else going on in my life had hit rock bottom. I was broken. It felt like I had lost it all. The past 8 years had been so confusing, most frustrating and extremely exhausting. People I loved and all the material assets I had worked so hard for, sacrificed so much for, were gone.

Losing my mom was shocking. No other way to explain it. My self-esteem and confidence were at an all-time low. I was stripped of my financial security, had lost my home, and losing my mom on top of all of that was the most painful experience ever. This was a dark time in my life. I lost my balance, was over-stimulated and my sense of hope was bleak. I was shattered.

Broken by what all of this was doing was crashing at the weight of it all. I had once again found myself in an unfortunate home situation and after moving four times in five months couldn't take it anymore. All of this was just too much to bear. I didn't know why this was happening. With having nowhere to go to, the only solution was to leave the city and head for solace elsewhere.

The environment we ended up in is beautiful, peaceful and we're surrounded by nature. Arriving here I knew it was the right choice. We've been coming here since I was 8 years old, grew up here, so this was like coming home. Exhausted and relieved to be here after the trauma experienced, the familiarity of it all was a gentle welcome relief.

After some time I realized how happy we are since leaving the city. We have nature, fresh air and quality time together. My daughter screamed with delight at the beautiful sunset, new rosebud or incredible full moon. Has the freedom to ride her bike when she chooses, play tennis, has a park to play in, snorkeling, rowing, fishing and swimming and a beautiful estuary and the ocean to choose from. All this time together has finally given me the opportunity to fully engage her, care for her and at the same time "teach" her. We have new-found love and appreciation for each other, the beauty of our natural surrounds and the wonder of it all.

Maybe it wasn't so crazy, to believe that maybe the doors in the city closed on purpose, to push me in a new direction. Had this not happened I would not have left, nor would we be here now.

Once I "got it" was willing to trust the process, endure the frustration, pain and confusion and continue on the journey knowing eventually it would all lead somewhere and finally make sense. Trusting and truly believing that it will, I worked hard at maintaining my faith. Through that time I discovered how supported and loved I was, no matter what, our needs have always been met which has made my faith stronger than ever. I finally found acceptance, learned the true art of humbleness and to let go completely, trusting and allowing events to unfold when they must.

I finally learned to go with the flow, live moment to moment, trusting and enjoying every experience and day for what it brought.

Of course, I asked "why" many times. Life was a battle. Financially I was no longer earning as I had left the city and needed to start afresh. Living in a small town, jobs were scarce, so hard to start afresh and find creative ways to bring funds in. Being human and having concerns of not being able to provide for my family panicked many times, yet you do what you got to do, and when times were really tough, and I plucked up the courage to ask for help, the support always arrived. Not only was this a really humbling experience, but also felt very loved and supported. My needs were always met. The more it happened, the more my Faith grew, the more I Believed, the more I Trusted. And of course I learned the true value of love and support, relationship with money, living in the moment and who and what truly matters.

"Who am I, What am I, Where am I going?

As time went by and things unfolded, I finally started to see the "bigger picture". It all suddenly started to make sense.

To know the "teachings", you have to know the "lessons".

The minute I committed to the journey I was also committing to learning the teachings and have to go through what I am going through to learn them.

If I hadn't gone through what I had gone through, I would not know what I know, nor would I be living here now, writing this book and sharing the knowledge.

What a revelation!
It all made sense. The dots were joining.

It was important to go through all the losses to finally find security within myself. Losing everything meant I had nothing to hold onto. I learned to trust myself more. I was given the tools and gained independence.

Once I knew what I wanted and had direction, the right people started entering my life, events unfolded and as time went by the path opened itself up to me and revealed itself.

Even though I thought I had a great idea to get the messages across when they birthed in 2002, little did I know how much hard work was still required. The time wasn't right, and I had much to learn. As I grew spiritually, the project evolved too.

It was all leading to this point and the start of something really beautiful.

All the teachings and lessons learned have been compiled together to create this book which has evolved into a "self-help owners handbook" over the course of 16 years. The book to serve as a reference point, as well as offer guidance as you expand your consciousness and embark on a journey of self-discovery.

Lessons are aimed at assisting you to understand life and how it works, the role you play and the importance of the written word and power of speech. Assistance in understanding why you are going through what you are going through and the tools provided so that you can change your experiences into positive experiences. Help you ask questions and identify who you are and what makes you tick. By knowing who you are and what you want, what makes you truly happy, what your passions are you will find your Purpose in life. When you commit to your Purpose and not focus on your earnings, when you love what you are doing, abundance will flow to you.

Imagine what a wonderful world we would live in should everyone find their purpose early in life. Imagine commencing your professional career doing what you love and are meant to do.

I may have experienced much pain losing all my material assets, however, have come to realize they were taken away from me for a good reason. Not only did they carry unnecessary weight, but they also did not align with my truth, my soul. I have lost so much, yet I have gained even more.

Through learning the lessons, walking the walk and doing the work have finally found my soul, my purpose. My heart has found its home. The pieces of my puzzle finally came together. At last everything finally made sense.

May the teachings shared help you as much as they helped me, and all of those who walked this journey before us, with us or after us.

Commit to your journey, have faith, trust, never give up and most of all, enjoy the experience it brings you. Remember the journey is what really matters. Your goal is simply your destination. Imagine telling "your story" to another, note how the conversation is based on "what happened" and not "what you got". The emphasis is always on the story of how you achieved your goal, ending with what you got as your reward.

Your transformation is the greatest gift you can give to yourself. Remember it's a process not to be rushed. Take your time with each chapter. There is no use in just knowing the theory you also have to do the practical. Walk the walk and talk the talk. Take action. Do the work. Remember, practice makes perfect.

Use the opportunity to re-define and re-invent yourself. Start with getting to know the basic rules of life. Work with each lesson for at least a week before moving on to the next. Go at your own pace so you can take it all in and most importantly have fun whilst doing it.

Enjoy the road to self-discovery. Be authentic.

Live a life of truth and love with a sense of purpose.

PREFACE

You must understand the whole of life, not just one little part of it. That is why you must read, that is why you must look at the skies, that is why you must sing and dance, and write poems, and suffer, and understand, for all that is life.
J Krishnamurti

Know thy self. Living by your truths will set you free. You'll find peace and live in a state of bliss. Life becomes effortless.

The purpose of this book is to empower you by giving you the tools you need to find your purpose in life, experience life to its fullest, help you to prosper. If you can change the way you think, you can change your world.

The power lies within you. The car you drive, the house you live in, the clothes you wear, your friends and associates do not define who you are. You have the power of choice.

You define who you are. You get to decide what kind of life you are going to live.

By teaching how to trust and listen to your inner voice so you can be guided by your Higher self.

By trusting that guidance, you will find your self guided to the right people, at the right time, for you to achieve your desires. These are your goals. This is your journey.

By learning to tap into yourself you become consciously aware of your thoughts and feelings. When you're aware of your thoughts and feelings you get to choose if you entertain them or if you don't like them, change them by thinking new thoughts. When you change the way you think and feel you bring about change to your inner world. By changing your inner world, your outer world will reflect the same.

You are responsible for the life you live. You are responsible for changing it. It all starts with you. It's your choice.

Your imagination is your preview of life's coming attractions.
Albert Einstein

To have it you have to be it. Act like you already experiencing it. Through intentions, affirmations, visualizations and paying attention to how you feel can manifest the things you want in life. Do the work and practice every day.

Finding your inner power will give you the confidence and strength to reach for your goals. You'll find the courage to face any situation you may find yourself in. Believing in your abilities and having the security of knowing you can take care of your self will make you happy. When you happy your life flows with much more ease.

By knowing your inner power, you can be content in the knowing you have what you need to reach your goals, and confident enough to reach them.

By being afraid of your strength, your inner power, you switch yourself off from your inner voice, disconnecting you from life and all it has to offer you.

The kind of life you live is your choice.

You can be average, never really excelling at anything or showing much interest in anything, never believing in anything, never willing to trust and take a leap of faith, you simply willing to settle, and live a life of non-existence.

Going through life simply existing from one day to the next can leave you feeling very alone, confused and disconnected.

This can leave you feeling like you need some love and validation. Others feel this need so pull back. The more you feel it the worse it gets making the situation go from bad to worse, leaving you with more reasons to feel unloved alone and in need of validation.

When this happens to you, little do you realize you are simply living your truths.

Every single thing you do it will get returned to you!

For every thought, spoken word and action taken is an action given to self.

Every word that is spoken is words said to self.

All the love and respect given to others is love and respect given to self.

Why it's so important to be impeccable.

Impeccable with your thoughts.
Impeccable with your words.
Impeccable with your actions.

Love your self.

Make choices that are best for you and in accordance with your Highest good. What is your Highest good?

What does your soul want? What will make your soul happy? What is best for you?

Is your life a true reflection of your authentic self and what you really value?

Why are you here? What are your gifts? What are you passionate about? What would nourish your soul?

Find your destiny.

Focus your attention on everything happening to, and around you. Be aware of the people you meet, the experiences had, and the opportunities that arise. These are your gifts. Appreciate them and be grateful for them.

This is your journey. Have an eye on your destination by knowing where you are going. This is your roadmap. Sit back and enjoy the ride.

Be present and go with the flow of your life. There's happiness to be found in the now.

You know what you want, trust in the timing of the manifestation. Let go of how and when you believe events should unfold and just appreciate every moment for what it brings.

To experience the magic and mystery of life pay attention to what's going on around you. There are always signs and synchronicities to inspire and guide you as you journey on your path of enlightenment. Know the moment you discovered the reason for your being here and made the conscious decision to follow your truths by setting goals or intentions, the journey has begun.

Trust in the Divine timing of your life. Allow events to unfold as and when they must. Transformation is a process that's not to be rushed.

Pay close attention to how you feel as that is your point of attraction. Stay positive and hold onto your faith. To have it you have to see it, feel it, be it. Keep your mind open and stretch yourself beyond your familiar to align with your dreams.

When you work hard and put your heart and soul into your work your wishes will be fulfilled in ways you never imagined. All it takes is tapping into the power of believing.

All the people that you meet, experiences you go through, all have a purpose to serve. There is no such thing as a coincidence. Looking back things always make sense in the end. You get to understand the reason why someone came into your life when they did, and why you've gone through what you've gone through.

No matter what you going through always look for the positive or what's to be gained from the experience.

Everything you go through grows you. All your experiences have molded you into who you are today. That's the very essence of who you really are.

Life is a journey. All that's required of you is to have fun and enjoy it. All your experiences are part of an exciting puzzle that will eventually fit together perfectly. This is the bigger picture. That is your destination.
It takes commitment, hard work, focus, and a strong desire to stay on your path. You'll be asked to make sacrifices and be of service to others.

When faced with an obstacle or challenge use your inner strength to push through. Find a way around it, over it, under it; do what you have to do to keep moving forward.

You'll experience many high's and low's, however this is all part of the journey of getting to really know you. Work with your emotions. The answers lie in how you feel.

Know thyself.

The purpose of the journey is to lead you down the path of self discovery to awaken you to your gifts. Let things happen organically instead of pushing for your way or forcing things to happen.

Always be true to self and don't forget to have fun. All that's required of you is to enjoy the ride.

If you think back to children's fairytales about the Prince who goes in search of his Princess, the journey he takes, the experiences, the challenges, frustrations and pitfalls and with determination finally slays the dragon, makes it to the castle and marries his Princess. It's such a great analogy as life is much like that.

When you want something you have to go out and make it happen. There will be challenges, times of frustration or pitfalls. Your commitment will be tested, but if you really want something you'll find the strength and courage to move through the obstacles to keep moving forward. If you can get through the challenges you will be victorious, you will reach your success.

You are here to evolve and grow. Accepting the lessons will help you overcome the challenges that stand in the way of your success.

To experience life at its fullest you have to appreciate there's duality in everything. You have to experience the negative as well as the positive to appreciate them both. If we did not know pain or discomfort we would not appreciate good health and contentment. If we did not know loss we would not appreciate the gains. Have to experience the highs, the lows, trials and tribulations to grow. Have to appreciate the disappointments as much as the joys, for without the disappointment you would not know joy.

Be grateful for the experiences gained, even if they did bring heartache, they also brought the gift of wisdom and growth which holds more power.

Use your discretion when choosing whom to share your time with. Be wise. If you want more positive experiences spend more time with positive people. If you want motivation spend time with motivated people. Be present. There's joy to be found in the now.

Take your mind off your concerns. Focus on what's right in front of you. Be in the moment and enjoy it for what it brings. Life will always show you where your attention is needed. When you trust in the flow of your life and tackle each challenge as it's presented to you, you'll find you manage with so much more ease as whatever needs your attention is getting it at the right time. Things just seem to work out. The right people will be in the right place at the right time to help you.

When faced with an obstacle remember it's only a challenge, is there to teach you something. See it for what it is. Try not to take it too personally. As much as your heart and mind is saying "oh no" your soul is rejoicing in happiness for the opportunity to grow. Take a step back, try to see the bigger picture, learn the lesson and let go.

Lessons are not there to punish or hurt, they are there to help you evolve and grow into your best self. Once you've got the lesson it simply goes away, but if you don't get it then "it" will keep coming back, each time harder than the last, until you do.

Live each moment to the fullest. Remove yourself from situations or people that don't have your best interest at heart, give more of your self to those that do.

Listen to your intuition. Pay attention to your feelings. Be conscious of your thoughts as your thoughts and feelings are what creates your reality.

When you wish for something make sure you really want it. Have fun and enjoy yourself as you learn and grow.

Be the master and leader of your own life.

There may be times when you really want something, have asked for it, yet haven't received it. With the flame of hope diminishing it's easy to feel defeated yet the minute you accept you don't have it, you stop giving it attention thereby letting it go. And that's when magic can occur. Out of nowhere, without any effort from you, something happens and you get what you asked for. Be it in the form of a gift of a career opportunity, more money, a new home or relationships, no matter what you asked for always trust everything that happens is in accordance with your Highest good in that moment of time.

By letting go of how you think events should unfold and when you think things should happen you allow the situation to unfold in the right way at the right time in the best way possible.

Sometimes you ask for something, and it doesn't come. Trust it isn't in accordance with your Highest good and there is something so much better out there for you.

Your soul knows what is best for you. Try not to be alarmed when you find yourself in situations where you totally overreact or respond differently to the way you normally do. Ever heard your self say, "Can't believe I reacted that way, I feel so stupid, oh why did I do it?"

Your subconscious guides you to make choices that are best for you. Listen to your intuition. Trust your Highest self. Know that even if things don't make sense now in due course they will.

Your happiness is your responsibility. Own your mistakes, apologize when needed, resolve any differences. Keep your conscious clear so you can focus on you. Be the best that you can be and see how your life takes on a whole new meaning.

Do all the good you can, by all the means you can, in all the ways you can, in all the places you can, to all the people you can, as long as ever you can.
John Wesley

Find reasons to be happy with where you are in your life right now, today. With utmost faith, confidently look at challenges as opportunities for growth. Let go feelings of fear or doubt, they only sabotage your efforts by creating obstacles that prevent or delay your progress.

Every time you get inspired with a new desire ask yourself "why?" "Why do I want that desire?" Holding your thoughts and feelings on that desire will keep you in the flow of Source energy which is the same energy as your desire.

Love yourself, all the aspects of your being. Extend that love further. Love everything around you, the people, the roads, the buildings, the plants and trees, the birds, the animals. See the gift of life and all it brings. Show your gratitude by never taking anything or anyone for granted.

We are all connected. One cannot survive without the other. Go beyond your own self-interests and think about the greater good of all. Blessed with a gift you are here to co-create with the Universe. Take responsibility for your part in the greater scheme of things and share your self with the world.

Abundance is your birth right. Have heaven on earth. Imagine what it feels like being in love, living a great life doing the things you enjoy, being abundant in every way. To know freedom and joy is when you're doing what you know you're meant to be doing.

Are your ambitions in line with what your soul wants to do? Do you have the courage of your convictions? Are you being authentic, true to you? Are you walking your talk?

Take the time, relax, and listen to your heart.

What is important to you? What really matters and would give your life meaning? What would fulfill your souls' needs?

To manifest something in your life it all starts with a thought. Pay attention to how it makes you feel. Once you can you visualize it, taste it, experience it, be it; follow through with action. You have to get the ball rolling. You have to make it happen. Set your intentions and get organized. Do the research, come up with a plan then get on with it always remembering to stay focused, grounded and true to you.

When faced with a road block find out what needs to be resolved so that you can release and let go, making space for what you do want to manifest. Everything you need to know is within you. Meditate, find your balance and go within. Let your inner voice be your guide.

As your inner life changes so your outer world will change too. You will start feeling and seeing the changes. Your confidence will improve your self-esteem goes up, inspiring you to maintain on your journey of self-discovery, and to live life with sense of purpose.

Believe. Trust and have Faith.

Your Creator wants you to be happy. When you trust your journey and follow the path that opens up for you everything that you need is provided for you when you need it. Your life flows. It's in accordance with your Highest good.

Your happiness is a priority. Every morning when you start your day make your dreams and goals your point of attraction. Ask for help with any issues you may have and set your intentions.

You have the gift of a new day filled with possibility. Visualize and feel your life as you would like it. Give thanks and be grateful.

Take it a step further and ask for help for others too. With compassion and understanding imagine a world at peace, where there's care and concern for this generation as well as the next. By doing so, you are cultivating empathy and compassion for all.

You are a powerful being filled with possibility. Believe in your self. Be courageous and confident by standing up for your self whilst at the same time learning the importance of being humble. Drop all sense of judgment so you can be there for others. Through kindness and generosity can shine your light into the world. Allow your joy to be seen by all.

Be the very best that you can be.

1 LOVE YOUR SELF

Be gentle with yourself, learn to love yourself, to forgive yourself, for only as we have the right attitude toward ourselves can we have the right attitude toward others.
Wilfred Peterson

To experience love it starts with you loving you. Instead of waiting for someone to give you the love you so desire, give yourself that love. That same love you give to others. Pamper yourself, spoil yourself, do the things you love. The love you have for you, others will give to you too.

Abundance is your birthright. Have heaven on earth. Feeling good lifts your self-esteem and increases your confidence making you happy. When you happy you attract more happiness.

Every moment in every day you have free will to make a choice. Love your self. Stop all sense of judgment or criticism toward self as well as others. There's nothing to be gained from the experience and only pulls you down in the process.

You are enough and perfect just the way you are. Forgiving yourself is just as important as forgiving others. Empower your self. Make space for something new and positive to come into your life. Move through the blocks by making a list of all your regrets and offer forgiveness to those that need it. Through love we find compassion, understanding, empathy and acceptance. With acceptance you'll find peace.

Where attention goes energy goes flows. Watch your thoughts. Your outer world is a reflection of your inner world. Pay attention to what you're thinking and feeling as you are creating more of that. The little thoughts you constantly think about will eventually develop into something bigger. Keep having loving thoughts and your world will reflect that back at you by bringing you more loving people and experiences to think about.

You are responsible for your happiness. Are the people, places and things in your life a true reflection of who you really are? When others show you feelings of jealousy, anger or simply don't like you, do you continue to allow them into your life for fear of being alone? You want to feel good about those that surround you as their energy and attitude can affect you in a myriad of ways without you even realizing it.

Love your self by surrounding yourself with positive and loving people. Give to others what you need the most and all that feel good energy will come back to you.

Positive energy brings positive outcomes. Negative energy brings negative outcomes.

The decision is yours. Every moment in every day you have free will to make a new choice. Are you connecting mentally, emotionally or spiritually? If the answer is no, then go where life takes you and wait until you do. All the experiences bring growth and a greater understanding of you.

When going through a tough time and things don't make sense, trust eventually they will. You are not a victim. Everything you go through you've chosen to go through on a deep soul level. As much as your heart is screaming "no" your soul is rejoicing in happiness for the growth. You will get to understand why you went through, what you went through, when you went through it. It always makes sense in the end.

Everything is as it should be. Don't beat yourself up for past mistakes. We've all done something we're not proud of and if given the opportunity would love to do it over again, but the past is gone, you cannot change it, the future hasn't happened yet. All you have is now. It's not about the mistake you've made it's your attitude toward it, and what you can do to fix it.

Be grateful for the gifts. See the beauty in the lesson as the experience has brought you wisdom and growth.

Always be honest and upfront when dealing with others and always consider their point of view. Tell them what you need and show them how you want to be treated.

Feelings of anger, regret and shame directed at others opens the door to your bitterness. When you hold a grudge it hurts you. Make a list of all your regrets, then forgive yourself as well as forgive others so you can heal and let go.

The changes start with you. De-clutter people, places and things that aren't loving, adding value or in your Highest good so that you can make space for people, places and things that do.

Take care of your own needs. Be true to you. Instead of seeking validation from others, seek validation from self. Make your health, happiness and peace a priority. If there is something that you've always wanted to do, now is the time to step up and do it. Eat nutritious meals, get enough rest, exercise, do what you love and don't forget to have fun.

Let the beauty of what you love be what you do.
Rumi

Know your worth. Surround yourself with those that love and reflect the true you. Set your expectations high and start taking care of your dreams. Find time in your busy schedule to do something that inspires and ignites the passion in you. When you're passionate about what you do you'll find the inner strength and drive you need to face the challenges, push through the obstacles and stay on your chosen path.

Filled with potential and possibility you are the leader of your own life. Anything you want You have to make it happen.

Love your self.

Don't let anyone stand in the way of your greatness.

Find your best self and always strive to be better.

2 RESPECT

Respect for ourselves guides our morals, respect for others guides our manners.
Laurence Sterne

The meaning of respect has different values in different cultures. Respect that. No one is better or more right, it is their truth. Respect and what it means to you is based on your beliefs, your upbringing, your experiences thereby creating your truths. Every culture has a different sense of value and worth, derived from how you treat me and how I treat you. It's a mutual response called respect.

What does respect mean to you, how does it feel for you?

Being respectful, authentically you, how you handle others, how you show up in the world, your values, your beliefs, your manners, your actions, all eventually become a habit based on your experiences and truths. No matter how much others respect you, what truly matters is how much you respect you. Confidence in self comes from knowing who you really are. When you know who you are can stand up for what you value, setting healthy boundaries and never compromising your integrity.

Respect you so that others respect you too. Know your boundaries, understand your limitations, be clear about what you willing to accept. Teach others how to treat you. The love, value and respect they have for you make it possible to set healthy boundaries.

If you want to be respected by others, the great thing is to respect yourself. Only by that, only by self-respect will you compel others to respect you.
Fyodor Dostoyevsky

We've all been through the unfortunate experience of being treated with disrespect. Our brains are wired to recognize when we're being disrespected as it's an emotional experience. All the painful experiences you've gone through have been banked to remind you so you don't go through them again. When it comes up again you recognize it, triggering the flight or fight response. When faced with a tough situation speak up. Say what needs to be said in a nice way. Actions or behaviors that damage or weaken an others spirit and sense of being, making them feel isolated and alone is showing disrespect. It's better to have honest conflict than give a false sense of harmony through dishonesty.

When an other is being disrespectful try not to instantly judge them. Look for greater understanding as the other may not realize they are being disrespectful as they come from a different culture with different beliefs. There is no one rule for all cultures. Should you find yourself in conflict, have the courage to walk away from those that cannot treat you the way you want to be treated with the respect you deserve. How you let others treat you is self respect.

If you want respect you have to give respect. Always treat people the same way you want to be treated.

When you do something that isn't a true reflection of who you really are or let yourself down in some way or another you just end of losing respect for your self. Pretending to be something you're not or getting jealous only makes you lose respect for your self.

You are enough. Be proud of who you are and what you stand for. Love all of you. Respect your self. Make choices that love you. When others do well, show your respect by giving them the credit when the credit is due. Be happy for them.

Take responsibility and own the choices that you make. Actions speak louder than words. Should you feel the need to criticize an other, respect they have feelings too. By offering constructive, loving advice they'll respect you for your kind thought full-ness instead of losing respect for you through your need to be critical or judgmental.

Understanding respect is helping us to fundamentally work more effectively and efficiently together.

We are all different and unique in our very own way. Respect others for their views, feelings and considerations and they will respect yours. Show your interest in their point of view by listening to what they have to say before offering a response. Their thoughts and opinions are just as valid as yours. Even if you don't agree, try to understand and respect where they are coming from and in return they will respect you for showing them respect.

Respect your dreams and the gifts you've been blessed with. When you true to you and your core values in life you'll have more respect for you.

The world we live in is a beautiful place. We have the gift of each other, the ocean, the mountains, the trees, the forests, the lakes, the rivers, plants and animals. Every one and every thing has a role to play in the bigger scheme of things. Even though we are all different we are equally important. Respect each one is as deserved as the other, and has the right to be here.

We must learn to live together as brothers or perish together as fools.
Martin Luther King, Jr.

No one is better than anyone else. No one is more superior or more deserved than anyone else. No one has the right to reject anyone or pass judgment. We all have our purpose, our roles to play and jobs to do. Each one forms part of a greater whole.

Give to every other human being every right that you claim for yourself.
Thomas Paine

Every spoken word, action taken is creating new life and movement. It's all energy in action. This is what makes our world go around.

Respect the earth, respect everyone living on it. Be conscious of the impact you make. Do what you can do to make a difference. No matter how big or small, do your bit.

To be one, to be united is a great thing. But to respect the right to be different is maybe even greater.
Bono

Own your power.

Take responsibility for the choices that you make.

Respect life and all that is in it. Be respect fully you.

3 HONESTY

You can fool some of the people all of the time, and all of the people some of the time, but you cannot fool all the people all the time.
Abraham Lincoln

There is immense power in being honest with your self. Standing in your truth takes courage and strength. Being honest means you get to know who you really are and willing to stand up for your truths. When you speak your truth, life flows effortlessly. Being in the flow of your life you'll feel balanced and happy. Life becomes joyous. Being in the feeling of joy it's easy to give joy to others and in return bring more joy into your life.

Be authentic. Always speak your truth and act with integrity. Being honest with self as well as others you're viewed as a trustworthy, dependable and reliable being. In return, you will attract dependable, trustworthy and reliable people into your life and experiences.

Honesty is always appreciated even if it's not shown to you right away. Once the reality, shock of the truth has settled, know no matter how painful the reality of that truth is, it's better as it's an honest response bringing you growth, offering expansion.

Be honest with your self. Should you be feeling unfulfilled in your job or your relationship, be not afraid to make changes. This is your life, only you get to live it and it's yours to enjoy. How you spend your time is up to you. You choose what you want, with whom and when.

Being honest with self as well as others brings its own rewards. Start with being true to you.

Being strong enough to be honest with your self, facing your self, isn't easy. It takes immense strength to admit you've been fooling yourself, helping you to figure out where you may have gone wrong.

It takes tremendous courage to be vulnerable with an other. Deception is a life long journey of learning to truly understand one self. Living a life of honesty is where the real freedom lies. There is no fear of retribution, or feeling the need to cover up. Being honest means you can 100% be you, get to express exactly how you feel in every moment, knowing it is safe as you never need to cover your tracks or look over your shoulder.

When you are dishonest with yourself and others, it doesn't feel good. You'll forget what you've said, and in response just end up adding more and more lies to the equation. Before long you'll forget what you've said and to whom. All the worrying can take up a lot of your energy can leave you feeling very uncomfortable for fear of being caught out.

When you make a choice that's not right for you, you'll feel it. Not feeling good about the choices and decisions you've made can burden you with feelings of disappointment. Sitting in that disappointment only leads to feelings of shame and despair. Feeling despair leads to more despair and so things go on. There's nothing to be gained from the experience, only loss of self respect, worry and despair.

When life becomes really challenging and difficult and you're left unhappy, confused and all alone, it's time to go within and ask questions of oneself. Are you being the best that you can be? Are you being the best toward self as well as toward others?

To get the most out of life, live a life of truth. Take the high road and always do what's right, even though it's sometimes more difficult and may require a sacrifice from you.

There is no pillow as soft as a clear conscience.
French proverb.

Being honest and living your truths takes hard work and commitment. It's not always easy to do the right thing, but in the end, it will always be worth it. You will always be glad you did. Hard work is always rewarded.

Taking the lower road is much easier, simpler, but that does not mean it's the right way. If taking the lower road means lacking in integrity in the choices that you make or being dishonest or inflicting pain on others, there won't be a positive outcome for you. What you put out you get back, bringing challenges, chaos, confusion or hardship, can leave you feeling depressed, unhappy about the choice that you made.

Being dishonest always comes at a cost. We are all masters of self deception. Not always willing or ready to face the truth or stick to the choices or commitments made, being dishonest about the smallest of details on a daily basis without even realizing it or acting in ways one couldn't admit to self, once you get to know you better, becoming more conscious and aware of these untruths gives you the opportunity to change them.

Honesty is good but sometimes the truth can also be painful. Make a point of carefully choosing your words whilst at the same time maintaining the truth. Being sensitive in the knowing that sometimes the truth can really hurt, being more tactful in your opinion is appreciated and avoids coming across as being offensive. Sometimes being kind is better than being nice. Even though the truth can be hard to hear, it may be necessary and in the best interest.

There is the right time to speak your mind and the wrong time to share your thoughts. Should an other be going through a difficult time, consider holding off the truth as a means to protect them. Offering your heartfelt affection and loving care whilst waiting for the dust to settle before exposing more truths will go a long way.

There is no such thing as a secret. The truth will out. People make mistakes. The truth always finds its way. Being honest with self is the key to living a peace full and happy life. Be true to you. Honor your feelings, even when those feelings make you feel uncomfortable. When you're honest with yourself will be easy to be honest with others.

Speaking the truth, even when it's uncomfortable, helps you to build solid and trustworthy relationships. When you respect others enough to always tell the truth will always get the truth in return. No matter what your circumstances, living a live based on truth and integrity brings just rewards. Many people, especially ignorant people, want to punish you for speaking the truth, for being correct, for being you. Never apologize for being correct, or for being years ahead of your time.

If you're right and you know it, speak your mind. Even if you are a minority of one, the truth is still the truth.
Gandhi

Transparency offers security. Knowing you are being truth full, always coming from a place of integrity and genuinely have the interest of others at heart, can lead the way in complete honesty.

Honesty builds trust. When you know someone is honest and always speaks their truth it forges a stronger bond in your relationships. Can really relax and enjoy your relations more as there are no hidden agenda's.

The underlying energy of complete honesty is refreshing. Speaking your mind is contagious, inspiring others to want to be more like you thereby contributing toward an honest and happy society.

4 FAITH

Faith is the light that guides you through the darkness.
Kenilworth Wisp

What is faith? Is it a belief? Is it both? Where does it come from? Why do we have it? Have you ever noticed when anyone uses the word faith no one ever asks what it means?

Just because you can't see it doesn't mean it isn't there. You can't see the future, yet you know it will come; you can't see the air, yet you continue to breathe.
Claire London

Faith is believing in something that is greater than you. What would a miracle be if you didn't have faith? How could your prayers be answered if you didn't have faith?

Faith is the confidence that what you wish for, will happen. It gives you assurance about things you cannot see. Having a relationship with your Creator means you trust and believe. It is this belief that strengthens your bond with your Creator and therein lies your power.

The smallest seed of faith is better than the largest fruit of happiness.
Henry David Thoreau

You have to know you have the power to create anything you desire. Have confidence and believe you do. When you speak, do it with conviction. Believe in you.

At times your faith will be tested. Be patient as patience gives your dreams and wishes time to manifest in the most perfect and unimaginable way possible.

Keep your faith strong. Trust your passions. Let life surprise you. Have faith no matter what happens the Universe always has your back. View challenges as optimistic opportunities to mature and grow. Be willing to take leaps of faith knowing and believing everything is going to be alright.

Have faith in your Creator. Have faith in self. Have faith in others.

You are the most important person in your life. Your soul knows what's best for you.

How often do we find ourselves in situations when you agree to an experience with others, knowing full well you actually already have arrangements and are letting someone else down, or when your friends desire an experience that you know is not what's best for you, or is morally wrong for you, or should you just not desire to spend time with others and prefer to stay home for a quiet night. Yet, you end up putting your feelings aside and go along with the others plans.

You'll experience many occasions where your soul wants to go in one direction, and others want you to make different choices and go in a different direction.

Love your self. Listen to your instincts. Listen to your heart. What does your inner voice say? It will guide you as to the best decision to be made in every moment at any given time. Trust you. Have faith that no matter what, you will always make the right choice. You are the director of your own life. You get to make the choices. You are responsible for the life you lead.

Have faith you will always be guided to the right people in the right place at the right time.

Have faith in your Creator. Ask for help and no matter what obstacle you're being faced with, show you trust that you will receive it. Let go. Believe, trust and expect things to work out.

Should things seem to be coming apart, and you feel like you're falling, let go and go with your flow. Trust the process. Know you are loved and supported, and everything will be okay. Just when you surrender and think things aren't going to work out for you, they do, restoring and strengthening your faith even more.

We all face storms in life. Some are more difficult than others, but we all go through trials and tribulation. That's why we have the gift of faith.
Joyce Meyer

There will always be a cushion for your fall. Imagine if there wasn't? No one would have faith and trust in the process. No one would believe.

Know that your Creator cares for you and wants to give you what's best for you. If you believe in this and have complete faith and trust, maintaining your commitment and willing to do whatever work is required, will be well rewarded; your life will be filled with much happiness, peaceful and secure in the knowing that no matter what, everything does, and will, always work out.

At times you wish for things and you don't receive them. Sometimes the things you wish for are not in accordance with your Highest good. Have faith that if you don't get what you want, something better for you will always transpire. You will be happy in the end.

How often in retrospect do you look at something from the past that you so truly deeply desired only not to receive it? At first you're devastated, angry, rejected but as time goes by you look back and realize with great relief it was better for you that you didn't get "it" as something went wrong there, and you were protected or you got something that ended up being much better for you and 100% nicer leaving you with no regrets. This will bring you even more joy than you believed you could have, and your faith will be restored yet again.

At times whilst in your darkest moments, and your faith is being tested, be strong. Never ever give up and always, always believe in you. Keep pushing through, face the challenges head on, there's self-betterment to be gained from the experience.

It's only fear of failure or loss that holds us back. Not taking action can lead to depression, being despondent to life. Face your fears. Life will always present you with challenges. That's how you learn and grow and evolve to a higher level of being.

Stress makes you believe that everything has to happen right now. Faith reassures you that everything will happen in Gods Timing.
Godvine.com

Know you always make the right choices and say the right things in that moment. No matter how strange or good they may have been at the time, trust yourself, or if you just can't see "it" it doesn't matter. We say and do all the right things at the right time, whether it's done on a conscious or unconscious level.

Stop stressing about situations gone by or how you could have done things differently. What's happened has happened. You cannot change it; it is in the past. Learn from it. Let it go.

Believe in yourself and never let faith go. Know the more anxiety you are experiencing, the tougher things are, the closer you are to reaching your goal. By trusting the process, keeping your faith, being optimistic, remaining positive, believing in your self, you will achieve your goals.

Be willing to face every situation as it arises. No matter what the reason was for your anxiety, know this too shall pass, and it's to be followed by a period of peace and joy.

Fear of, will simply dissipate.

5 TRUST

The best way to find out if you can trust somebody is to trust them.
Ernest Hemingway

Trusting self is the first step in gaining trust. If you trust you, others will have reason to trust you too.

You have been gifted with an inner voice, called your sixth sense. No matter how you identify with it, get to know you. Listen to your inner voice.

You have permission to walk away from anything that doesn't feel right.
Trust your instincts and listen to your inner voice. It's trying to protect you
Bryant McGill

Once you pay attention and listen to yourself combined with being consciously aware of what's going on around you, you will "hear" the answers that you seek, helping you, prompting you so you know what you need to say or do as you take steps every day.

Depending on whether you are excited or distressed, you will note your voice sounds like it has two different tones.

One tone is higher pitched, comes to you when you are in a frenzy, when you are under duress, when you are angry, rejected, upset, etc., and the other is a softer, calmer, deeper pitched voice that comes to you when you are still, being quiet, relaxing, out in nature, driving on a long trip, dozing off, cooking, etc.

Let's call the two voices, the voice of fear and the voice of reason. The deeper, calmer voice is your instinct, your voice of reason, your Higher mind. The higher pitched, scared voice is your unconscious voice of fear, representing your ego, your Lower mind.

Learn to discern between these two voices.

Confidence is silent. Insecurities are loud.
Joel Osteen

Have fun and play with it. For example, you are out with friends and have an exam in the morning that you have been working really hard for and a friend suggests you go out to a party. Your higher pitched voice says, "Oh gosh I know it's taking a chance but I'm going, it'll be so much fun and who cares about that exam anyway, have been working hard, oh my goodness, deserve a little fun".

Your lower pitched voice of reason comes in and says "You've worked so hard for so long, why go and throw it all away now? Why don't you get the exam over with and then go out and celebrate with your friends? You'll feel so much happier and enjoy it so much more knowing you gave it your all."

Listen to your self. Feel your way through. Deep down you know which choices are the right choices for you. Trust your Higher mind, your intuition, your instincts, and go with what your voice of reason is telling you to do.

Making choices and decisions whilst under pressure is sure to disappoint you. Don't give in to the pressure of the voice of fear. Think about things, feel what your heart wants and trust you will know what to do, when, and how to do it.

Pay attention to how you feeling, the energy you're giving off from the moods you may find yourself in. Then pay attention to what your inner voice is saying and thinking. Is the rambling going on in your mind affecting your mood?

You'll notice a calm feeling when happy about the decisions and choices you are making, and you will notice a feeling of unease when making choices that are not best.

By tapping into your sub-conscience, you learn to really listen to yourself. You know, have and hold all the answers to the questions you seek. You only have to go within to find them. Your heart always knows what's best.

When facing a situation in your life, stop and pay attention. Think about your experience and what's going on. Feel the situation and listen. By giving yourself the time and space needed to think about things, contemplate your situation, you will feel what the right course of action must be, as well as you will get the affirmations you seek, be it from how your choice makes you feel to some other affirming it to you.

When making choices with calm emotions, from the "heart and mind", you will feel you can trust the choice you have made so can act on the information with confidence.

Always trust that you have made the right choice for your self in that moment of time even if it doesn't appear that way. If you trust yourself and act on the information you are guided to, you will make the right choices.

You will not only receive information through your Higher mind you are also helped along the way by little messages that pop up. The people you encounter. Could even be the odd message received from the stranger standing next to you in the queue whilst shopping, or the headline that catches your eye whilst browsing the latest magazine or the synchronicity of the movie you are watching, or the song playing on the radio.

Signs are everywhere to help you.

What's important to note is the messages come through in all forms. Pay attention as they can come in strange and amazing ways; or they could simply come as words of wisdom from someone you value and love.

Trusting completely that you are guided, you only have to be consciously aware and open to listening to every thing and every one all around you.

For example; you are under immense pressure as you have loads of work to do, so you find yourself rushing around, running yourself ragged because you have so many problems that desperately need sorting out and you just don't have any time for this, you want it all sorted out now.

Pushing for your way may not always be the right way for the situation on hand. As a result may find yourself being subjected to all sorts of new obstacles and challenges only amplifying the problems you already have.

When you feel the need to be in control you are showing you do not trust you will get the help that you need when you need it. You don't trust that everything will work out. You feel you have to be in control of the situation in order to succeed.

Where attention goes energy flows. Whatever you give your attention to it expands and grows thereby giving you more of the same, only resulting in unnecessary frustrations or delays.

Trust. What's meant for you always comes effortlessly. All you need to do is know what you want, ask for help, then let go in faith, trusting you will receive it.

Sometimes help comes from the most unsuspecting sources. Don't question it. Just go along with it, be flexible. Know that everything is perfect and always makes sense in the end.

People, information, the situations you may find yourself in, are all stepping stones to guide you as you walk your path, helping you to take care of matters along the way. No matter the shape or form your guidance comes in, trust the outcome will always be in accordance with your Highest good.

Be still. Ever present in every way, live in the moment. Savor each second for what it brings. True power lies in the present, can see opportunities as they come up, giving you the option to utilize them to your utmost benefit.

I trust that everything happens for a reason, even when we're not wise enough to see it.
Oprah

Trust you. Trust your Creator. Trust everything always works out. Trust you will be in the right place at the right time. Trust the delays. Trust the madness. Trust everything is perfect and as it should be. Trust what's meant for you will come to you. Trust you will receive it.

6 KINDNESS

Kind words can be short and easy to speak, but their echoes are truly endless.
Mother Theresa

A little extra kindness goes a very long way. Whatever you give you get back. By giving to others, you are essentially giving to your self. Kindness starts with you.

Choose to love your self. Be kind to your family and friends. Appreciate them for all that they bring. Choose to help others. Get to know your neighbors; you never know how much your visits can mean to them as well as how knowing them can improve or impact on your life until you spend time and are interested in them. Choose integrity compassion and understanding. No matter how great your successes in life, true success lies in how well you treat others.

Be kind to the old lady needing to cross a busy street. Help her get across. You will feel great as you have just given of your self, and seeing the appreciation on her face will fill you up with feelings of great joy.

Unexpected kindness is the most powerful, least costly, and most underrated agent of human change
Bob Kerrey - American Politician

That feeling is rewarding itself; it will lift you. You will feel a rush of energy circulating in your body, filling your cells. This rush of feeling feels good, will make you happy, your face will shine, your smile will be real and full. You'll feel energized and look fantastic.

When you feel great you give off lots of positive energy and in return attract others to you. When others want to be with you, you'll feel it, and this will make you feel good about your self. Feeling good about yourself will lead to you feeling good about others and wanting to do things for them by giving of yourself and treating everyone kindly. When being kind to others, others are kinder to you and in return will make you kinder to more and more people and in return, more and more people will be kinder to you, and so it goes.

Where attention goes energy flows. Whatever you focus on and give your attention to you are creating more of that in your life.

Be kind to your pets. They too need your love and support. By being kind and caring they will love you and look after you and always be loyal to you in return.

Be kind to the animals. They too have important roles to play. Be kind to the earth and the earth will look after you. It will feed you, support and provide for you. It will nurture you.

Get to know your self. Be gentle and kind. Treat yourself the same way you treat others. Need more love? Give more love and that love will come back to you. Always give to others what you need the most.

One day when you pass away are people going to talk about how much money you made or are they going to talk about who you are, your values, your integrity, what you stood for, and how well you treated others?

The difference we make in the lives of others will always be remembered. The joy you feel in return will always be remembered. It's a win/win feel good situation. Everyone benefits.

Who you are is so much more relevant than what you have. The true meaning of success is how you make others feel. In a world that is fraught with difficulty making someone feel good goes a very long way. Be kind. Choose to be the change you wish to see in the world. Decide. Set the example for others to see. Helping an other feel good will help them help an other feel good too. It's energy in motion.

Never really knowing what's going on in the life of an other, one small act of kindness can turn a life around. You never know the power behind a small gesture. Be the reason someone makes a difference in the life of others, the domino effect.

Always do what is right, not what is easy in the moment. No one has ever become greater by making another smaller. Treat everyone with the same level of kindness. Treat everyone the same way you want to be treated.

Give your self a reward when you achieve something or do something great. Take the time to pat yourself on the back and savor the moment. You deserve it. Celebrate the small victories that lead to bigger goals. Allow all that feel good energy to flow through your body. Sit in the feeling of what it feels like. Let all that positive energy nourish you.

Your physical body is the vehicle for your soul. Listen to it. Love, protect and nourish it. Give it what it needs. If you don't feed and take care of it, you won't have the energy to go anywhere or do anything. Just like a car cannot run without petrol you too need breaks to nourish your body, rest and recharge.

When you are healthy, your body and mind can function at your highest level. You find yourself making the right choices. You're productive and able to get things done with ease. Getting things done will make you feel good, invigorated, inspired and satisfied with your self. This raises your sense of self-worth and increases your confidence. You'll feel like you've achieved something.

When you're feeling good, you're giving off feel good energy. It's easier to be kind and generous towards others. When you are happy, you will extend your happiness on to others. When you are feeling good, you are helping others feel good. When you are kind, you are helping others find kindness. Treat others the same way you want to be treated. By being kind and thoughtful toward your self as well as others, you in return will be showered with kindness and thoughtfulness.

A kind and gentle spirit desiring to leave this world in a better place is where your greatness lies.

7 RESPONSIBILITY

The true essence of responsibility is the ability to respond.

Being responsible for the state of your consciousness determines the life you create.

It all starts with you being responsible towards you.

The world you create the actions you take and the consequences of those actions.

Own your life. Take responsibility for what you want to create.

No one is going to take responsibility for you. No one is going to give you permission to live your life to its fullest. It's all up to you.

Be responsible. Have response-ability toward your self, others, our planet and everything else surviving on it.

By taking responsibility for your self you are ultimately contributing towards a greater society. We all form part of a much bigger picture, together we become part of a greater whole. We all have the ability to respond.

Responsibility is not inherited, it is a choice that everyone needs to make at some point in their life.
Byron Pulsifer

The change starts with you. It's a transformed state of consciousness.

Take responsibility by making life happen instead of waiting for life to happen.

Allow your self to be different. Don't just accept things the way they are. Don't let circumstances from the past define who you are now, nor allow people, events, experiences define who you're going to become.

Embracing and accepting it all is what propels you forward.

Life is not about existing, it's about living.

First and foremost is taking ownership of who you are becoming.

Be responsible. If you say you'll be somewhere, be there. If you say you're going to do something, do it. Be a person of your word. Own up when you have done wrong. Taking responsibility when you have done something wrong is the first step toward doing it right. It's not how you messed up. It is about how you fix the mess up.

We are all human, we all make "mistakes". Those mistakes are there to teach you. There is no such thing as a wrong choice or a mistake.

Sometimes you do things without giving it much thought.

On a conscious level you would never normally do "something", yet for some or other reason you are stressing out as you did that "something" and you can't understand what came over you. You question your choice and scold yourself for doing "it". Even though something may look like a mistake at that moment, in the long run, it may just turn out to be your blessing in disguise.

Every choice made, be it on a conscious or unconscious level, and every action taken, will bring you a gift, the gift of knowledge and learning something new.

It could even be a gift of teaching you something about yourself, or the gift of inner strength gained from the experience.

Take a step back and try to see the bigger picture. Go inside yourself and know that within every painful situation lies a gift in return.

"There's a silver lining in every cloud".
John Milton

Look for it and appreciate it, even if it's caused you pain. Trust that there's a reason why you are learning this "lesson" in this moment. Rather learn the lesson and go through the pain with a situation that isn't "right" for you, so that you are prepared for the one that is.

Be grateful for the growth.

All the experiences you go through, the trials and errors, the highs the lows, the people you meet and the experiences had, loves gained and lost, death of loved ones, no matter what it is that you are going through, all of it is molding you into the person you are becoming today.

Find a way to be grateful and happy for the one that provided the experience, no matter how much anger, resentment, pain you may have gone through.

When you take on a job or work on a project, love your self.

Loving your self is being responsible by being trustworthy and dependable, always arriving on time and doing the work that is required of you to the very best of your ability.

By committing and fully engaging yourself with what you are doing in that moment, you will always love what you are doing, and you will do it well.

By being responsible, your efforts will be noted, and in return, you will be well rewarded for all your dedication and hard work.

Receiving recognition makes you feel good. Feeling so good will spur you on to continue to work hard, so that you can continue to gain recognition. You'll feel affirmed.

The more responsible you are, the more responsibility will be handed to you. This will bring more new experiences and more experiences to enjoy.

Should you feel there is more to life than what you're currently experiencing, believe that there is.

We all have very specific "jobs" to do, why we are here. No matter how big or small, they are all equally important. You have to reach out and make things happen. You have to take leap of faith and jump into the unknown. Every dream will become a reality in return there is a sacrifice to be made. Every day you have to wake up, committed to doing the work to make it happen. Then you work, work and keep working until you do.

Accept yourself, your strengths, your weaknesses, your truths, and know what tools you have to fulfill your purpose
Steve Maraboli

Know that the choices and decisions you make affect others. We are all connected. We all form part of a greater whole. Be responsible when making those choices.

Every time you make a choice think of it as if you're throwing a pebble into a pond. The pebble drops, causes a splash followed by waves, "the ripple effect". The reaction and results from that choice.

It goes beyond you. Always consider how it could affect you and/or those around you.

Own your Life.

Be conscious of everything around you by being responsible for all the choices and decisions you make.

8 APPRECIATION & GRATITUDE

Our goal should be to live life in radical amazement... get up in the morning and look at the world in a way that takes nothing for granted. Everything is phenomenal; everything is incredible; never treat life casually.
Abraham Joshua Heschel

Every emotion, every feeling carries a vibration.

With love and gratitude vibrating at the highest frequency start your day by appreciating what you have and list the things you are grateful for. Do that every morning and watch how your list grows.

You'll feel good. Because you feel good you'll look good. Because you feel and look good you'll radiate with confidence and joy.

A peace full mind and a peace full heart is the key to your happiness. You can attract miracles and abundance through the sheer power of gratitude.

There's magic to be found in believing.

Feel gratitude. Hold onto that feeling wherever you go. Make it your point of attraction and see how fast your list to be grateful grows.

Be grateful for the solar system, our planet and all that inhibit it. Be grateful for the sun, moon and the stars; our trees, rivers and seas; the fauna and flora, insects, birds and sea life.

Be grateful for your parents, your siblings, your loved ones, friends and those you call family. Show your mom how much you appreciate her. Tell her how wonderful she is and how much you love her and why.

When your dad works long hours to provide for the family show him how much you appreciate him. Tell him how much you love him, how much you appreciate him for working so hard to look after the family.

Tell your friends and family how much you love and appreciate them for being in your life. The joy and beautiful experiences they bring to you.

Even when the going gets tough, and you're fighting, appreciate them.

Never stop loving them.

Imagine what life would be like without them.

Love unconditionally. Remember once they are gone you can never tell them how special they are or how much you love and appreciate them.

Be grateful for your pets and the joy they bring.

Be grateful for the things you value the most. Be grateful for what really matters.

When you receive help, show your appreciation; when you have a great day, show appreciation; when you're learning something, show appreciation; when you get rewarded, show appreciation. Show appreciation for the opportunities received, for the love and support. Be grateful and appreciate everything you have.

Gratitude bestows reverence, allowing us to encounter everyday epiphanies, those transcendent moments of awe that change forever how we experience life and the world.
John Milton

Take your focus off what you don't have and appreciate everything you do have.

Being grateful is the key to your happiness.

The more you appreciate what you do have, the more reasons you will be given to appreciate what you have.

When you need something and receive it be gracious and have gratitude. Thank that person for what they have given you, show your appreciation.

It will nurture them and in return will nurture you too.

Appreciate everything in your life. Find reasons to be grateful for what you have got.

Be grateful for the food you eat, clothes you wear, bed you sleep in for there are many out there who aren't as blessed.

Be grateful for and appreciate your ability to study, your career, your home, money in the bank for there are many out there who aren't as blessed.

Appreciate nature, the outdoors and how much it means to you.
Be grateful for the lovely weather and warm nights.
Appreciate the buildings and the roads.
Be grateful for the car you drive or transport you rely on.
Appreciate running water when you turn on your taps, or the electricity to turn on your lights.
Appreciate the internet and how it helps you to stay connected.
Appreciate your body, your health, your sight, your hearing, your limbs.

Appreciate the moments and be grateful for those you can share it with.

Living a life of gratitude and appreciation brings peace.

Before long you will find yourself in a happier state of being. You'll feel more positive and happy. All this happiness brings on more reasons to feel joy and for nice things to keep happening to you.

Whilst you enjoy life, always remember those who were there for you and supported you by helping you when you were down.

Be responsible and gracious.

Never compare your self to others.

There will always be an other who has more than you. Finding joy in the now and willing to give of your self will help you forget about what you don't have.

Be grateful for what you have got and appreciate those who assisted you in getting it.

Wealth is not measured by the car you drive or the house you sleep in and how much money you have in the bank.

Wealth is measured by your happiness, your successful relationships with family and friends, the amount of love and support you have in your life.

Be conscious of the gifts you receive and show gratitude.

By doing it again and again, day after day, you'll become more aware and notice how much more you have to be thank full for.

Remember by giving thanks every day you'll have so much more to give thanks for every day.

Every morning start your day by being grateful to be alive, for a new day that is filled with the gift of potentiality.

Be thank full in advance for the gifts the day is going to bring.

Be gracious for your experiences, for they have made you who you are today.

Be gracious by showing your gratitude and appreciation for all that you are, have been and will be.

Be thank full for another day just to be you.

9 COMMUNICATION

Words are singularly the most powerful force available to humanity. We can choose to use this force constructively with words of encouragement, or destructively using words of despair. Words have energy and power with the ability to help, to heal, to hinder, to hurt, to harm, to humiliate and to humble.
Yehuda Berg

Be very mindful of what you're feeling, thinking or saying.

Pay attention. Spend a day focusing on your thoughts and choice of words. Find a quiet spot, let your mind wander and for half an hour write down everything that comes to mind.

How much is time spent in thought or speech is constructive? How much is mindless banter, and how much is uplifting, positive, loving and compassionate and how much is negative, fearful or ego-based?

Take a good look at your life. How many thoughts have come true, have manifested and how much time went by before they did.

You're constantly stressing you won't be able to pass your exam. Day in and day out you revisit the negative situation, spending time thinking about how much you don't know and how much you still have to do. You fear you are going to fail your exam. You fear you are going to get questions you don't know anything about. You see it playing out in your mind. You feel the pain of failure; you imagine yourself failing. This makes you even more anxious. You tell your friends, you talk about it so much, and stress about it so much you start believing it. By the time you go to write the exam you have put so much energy and time into how you are not going to pass the exam, and so you don't. Guess what? Everything is exactly the way you imagined it would be.

Once you're consciously aware, you will quickly note how easily you can manifest your hopes and fears. Remember whatever you feel, think or say you are manifesting it. Where attention goes energy flows. It is energy in action.

Imagine a word or thought being carried in a big bubble floating through the air. The bubble pops, the thought or word is airborne. The thought or word carries energy, upon its release it's ready to be manifest.

Speak clearly, if you speak at all; carve every word before you let it fall.
Oliver Wendell Holmes, Sr.

When you realize the power of this, and the importance of it, you'll realize the importance of being thoughtful.

Always have impeccable thoughts, feelings and use impeccable words. For in the end those thoughts, feelings and words define your life's experiences. Whatever you put out comes back to you. The boomerang effect.

Walk your talk. Whatever you say you are going to do, do it. See it through to completion. This will leave you feeling immensely satisfied as you'll feel you've accomplished something raising your confidence and self-esteem.

What you feel, think and say, you create.

Be very mindful of what you're feeling, thinking and saying, all day, every day as that is your point of attraction.

Once you become conscious of your thoughts and start paying attention as to how much of it is mindless banter and how much is positive, you can easily change it.

Let go of mindless clutter, bantering and negative thoughts. When they pop up, simply drop them by thinking about something else. Use your time wisely by entertaining positive thoughts and actions.

Be the silent watcher of your thoughts and behavior. You are beneath the thinker. You are the stillness beneath the mental noise. You are the love and joy beneath the pain.
Eckhart Tolle

If a negative thought comes into your mind banish it, don't even entertain it. Just drop it. By giving it attention you are "feeding it". Every time you feed it you give it more energy than it had before, therefore giving it more power and helping it become a reality.

For every negative thought or feeling you have, you are sabotaging your self.

You are simply delaying the process, and creating obstacles on your path that were never there, thus blocking you from achieving your goals.

When you complain about others, speak behind their back you are creating the situation for an other to do the same to you.

Should you find yourself in a situation with an other, and they are negative, speaking ill of, complaining about, and saying horrible things about another, by joining in the conversation you are connecting with their energy, attracting "that" to happen to you too. There will be an other who too will say these things about you. The boomerang effect! Everything you say or do, it will get returned to you!

As soon as you find yourself entertaining a thought or feeling that does not benefit you, let it go. Use your mind constructively. Use it for visualizing. Use it for creating positive thoughts and feelings. Follow through with action.

Being thoughtful allows you to focus on your thoughts and feelings. Giving focused energy to your thoughts and feelings results in the quick manifestation of those thoughts and feelings.

Practice makes perfect. You'll learn to master energy through your thoughts, words, and feelings.

10 COMPETITION / CONFLICT

One of the greatest challenges we face in life is conflict. What is it that makes conflict so difficult? No matter who you are, or where you are in life, there will always be a reason for conflict. Your challenge lies in your willingness to fix it.

Competition brings out your best and unleashes your passion and commitment in what you believe in.
Sonia Choquette

Conflict is the result of one's needs not being met. When the other is unwilling to meet those needs it causes conflict. Many times it acts as a catalyst as deep within you is something you are not speaking up about. No matter how big or small the conflict creates a situation where you are forced to open up and speak from the bottom of your heart. This is good as you'll express yourself with pure emotional truth and passion.

Seek compromise so you can find a way for both parties to be happy. Sulking, seeking vengeance, talking about them behind their back, being angry are all emotional responses to your needs not being met, making you vulnerable. Instead of reaching out and speaking about it, opt instead to withdraw from the other, resulting in an unexpressed need only needing to be expressed again later.

Handling conflict resolution from a place of maturity, love and understanding will find a solution that's best for all concerned. Try to take the long view, look for the positive in the situation. Why has the conflict happened in the first place? What is it about the conflict that's so difficult to face for you?

What can you do, what contribution can you make to fix it?

Conflict isn't a bad thing. It gives you an opportunity to express how you truly feel as well as affirms what it is you really want or believe in.
Deep down at the core of your being lie your truths. Simply walking away, being unwilling to face the other just to avoid conflict, adds more conflict and emotional stress lasting days, weeks, months or even years.

When faced with conflict take a step back. View it from all sides before coming to a conclusion. Reach for understanding so you can clear up any misunderstandings. Discuss matters calmly by openly discussing the issues you have and why you are upset. Never leave it hanging. The more time it takes to sort the issue out, the longer you are in pain, making it all the more difficult to sort out. The discomfort you experience during that time can leave you feeling anxious.

Sometimes talking about the conflict can only make matters worse. Learning the art of compromise is the key to finding resolution. Take a step back to regain your balance. View your situation from afar. Suspend all judgment until you have a clear understanding of the situation on hand. You know you've reached a positive conclusion when there's a win/win for all concerned.

Conflict shouldn't be seen as a bad as it provides a solution where there was none. You're given the opportunity to speak about everything that is bothering you and express how you truly feel. You speak your truth. See the beauty in that as it creates change in the circumstances that surrounded you causing the disharmony.

If you really want to live your life to the fullest and realize your greatest potential, you must be willing to run the risk of making some people mad. People may not like what you do, people may not like how you do it, but these people are not living your life – You Are!
Iyanla Vanzant

Competition is good. It unleashes your passions and makes you stand up for you and what you want, affirming your values and beliefs. It makes you stronger preventing others from taking advantage of you. It also teaches respect for self as well as others, a reminder never to impose your will on them.

With conflict comes respect and responsibility. It reminds you of what really matters. At times of inner turmoil try to work out what it is that's bothering you. What is your soul trying to tell you? What are you being alerted to? At times of feeling stuck you'll be faced with inner conflict causing discomfort and pressure, pushing you forward and out of the situation.

Conflict is a wonderful thing. Without it there would be no heartfelt conversations giving you the opportunity to get to the core of how you really feel, letting you get to the root of the problem by expressing those feelings.

No matter what the challenges are and what you have to face, face it, there is a reason why you are going through what you are going through and with the other. Reach for understanding instead of pushing to get your own way or to simply win the fight.

At times when you feel you're not responsible for something that has occurred; consider the conflict has been put there to show you there is an issue that needs your attention. Be honest with yourself. Be willing to face your shortcomings or contributions in causing the conflict. Being irresponsible and not owning the choice you've made only keeps you stuck in repeating the same patterns, holding you in the past and never moving beyond it.

Getting to the core of how you really feel helps you to root out the problem. Digging deeper within yourself helps you in recognizing where you may be wrong, thereby opening the doors to finding a solution.

To have change in the outer world it starts with making changes to your inner world. It's all up to you. It takes strength and vulnerability to admit when you've been wrong. Being vulnerable removes the blame from others helping you to own the choices that you've made bringing unity where there was only conflict.

Whenever you're in conflict with someone, there is one factor that can make the difference between damaging your relationship and deepening it. That factor is attitude.
William James

Taking ownership, being accountable, recognizing your needs, your choices, your decisions all define your outcomes.

Owning those choices, making good decisions is the first step in moving past the conflict.

Ask for what you want.

Be willing to really listen to what the other has to say. Express how you feel and don't concern yourself with how the other is going to receive it. You have no control over how others are going to respond or react. All you can do is focus on self.

Asking tough questions of one self, being willing to listen to your heart and face your truths is the first step to be taken to finding a solution. Where am I going wrong, what role did I play to cause the conflict and what can I do to make it better?

To reach a successful conclusion all parties need to want a resolution. Accept what you can change, embrace what you cannot. How others respond is out of your control. Focus on how you feel without worrying how the other will receive it. Keeping the communication open and honest builds stronger relationships, setting the foundation for trust.

At times it's hard to stand up for yourself, choosing to please others to keep the peace or not rock the boat to maintain a sense of popularity. Being willing to engage in difficult conversations will gain you the respect that you deserve.

Through self examination given the opportunity to repair or remove what isn't serving you. The more you invest in your relationships, the more you have to lose, making you vulnerable. Lead with compassion. With understanding can reach resolutions.

You are the leader of your own life. Stand up for your self. Fight for what you believe in. Be responsible and willing to own up to your faults.

The change starts with you.

11 POSITIVE OUTLOOK

Successful people maintain a positive focus in life no matter what is going on around them. They stay focused on their past successes rather than their past failures, and on the next action steps they need to take to get them closer to the fulfillment of their goals rather than all the other distractions that life presents to them.
Jack Canfield

By maintaining a positive outlook, you'll find yourself living a positive life.

The key to having whatever your heart wants or desires is finding a way to feel good about everything. Look for the positive within every situation.

When you are joyful, when you say yes to life and have fun and project positivity all around you, you become a sun in the center of every constellation, and people want to be near you.
Shannon L. Alder

Instead of "needing" it and "wishing" for it and not feeling good about "it" because you don't have "it" change the way you feel. Imagine and feel yourself receiving "it", having "it", being "it". Feel good about it. By feeling good about it, you have started the process of creating it.

When you need it, you are coming from a place of fear, by wanting or desiring it you are coming from a place of passion, joy and excitement.

You find yourself in lack. You don't have enough funds to get you through the month. You spend a lot of time thinking about what you don't have and what you do need. You spend a lot of energy worrying thus drawing in more of the very things you are lacking, a lack of funds to support your needs. So the cycle of lack continues, and the flow just gets bigger, and so do your problems, they just seem to grow and grow.

Now you're being faced with not only lack of finance, but it also impacts on your social life of fun, friends, food, and comforts. The flow of lack is flowing strongly around you; you spend all your energy thinking about it, leaving no time to figure out what you do want, or even how to get it.

Thus feeding the "lack" cycle even more.

By simply feeling positive about the situation, no matter how dismal or big it may appear at the time, by staying focused on what you want to achieve, always believing and trusting that all will end well, you will be guided to the right people at the right time. There will be a positive outcome because you are positive and you are creating that.

Once you replace negative thoughts with positive ones, you'll start having positive results. Willie Nelson

All it takes is 16 seconds of focused feeling to create what you want. When you want something specific, hold your thoughts and focus on that. What does it look like? What does it feel like? Does it make you feel excited and happy?

When you're feeling excited and happy you'll feel positive about everything, and suddenly life will become exciting. Wonderful prospects start to pop up, you'll notice there are opportunities everywhere.

On the other hand all it takes is 16 seconds of dwelling on a situation that makes you feel low and depressed to feed it, get it going, blowing everything out of proportion creating a mountain of new challenges, giving you more reason to feel low and depressed.

It's all about your thoughts. When faced with a crisis how much time is spent visualizing a positive outcome and how much time is spent revisiting the event, going over it again and again making you feel more anxious?

When you're feeling low, you're thinking about not having, that's poverty consciousness. When you're feeling positive, you'll feel abundant, may find yourself expressing gratitude and appreciation.

Once you know what you want, you must find the feeling of what it's like to live your want and be "it". Act like its already there. Work hard at holding onto those feelings. At times you'll feel challenged by the thoughts of not having "it", letting doubt set in. When negative thoughts come up, don't entertain them, don't give them any energy.

You really need to get good grades as your Dad has promised to reward you with a skiing trip with your best friends. You are desperate to join your friends on their holiday. You dream about it. You see yourself skiing down the mountain with all your friends around you, all having a really great fun time, sharing much laughter and joy. But then suddenly your dream comes crashing down, you remind yourself that you will not be living this dream if you don't make good grades. Now, this concerns you. Oh dear, what if I didn't do it, what if.. what if.... All the positive energy gained from living the joyful experience is lost and replaced by fear and negative energy of what if.

When you're feeling excited, you're a magnet for more exciting experiences. You'll enjoy life, are positive, so you start drawing in more positive energy which impacts on your life with more positive experiences. Things will start going your way.

Positive opportunities will always be present for you to achieve your goal. There are steps to be taken. This is your journey. This is how your desires unfold.

Feel. Get excited about your desires and what it would be like to be living your dream.

See and feel yourself attaining your goal, experience the moment. Sit in the feeling.

See yourself celebrate, feel the joy. Allow the good energy to flow through your body, nourishing you as it moves through you. Keep your vibration up by seeing your life after your dream has unfolded. Now that you have it, what are you going to do now?

You have good grades; you can go on your trip. Don't end there. Go beyond the good grades. See yourself confirming excitedly to your friends. Feel the excitement. See yourself packing. Feel the joy of it. See yourself flying over. Feel the excitement of leaving. See and feel yourself enjoying your time and what you get up to whilst you're there. See and feel yourself coming back. Now what? See yourself after that. Keep seeing yourself going forward and feel what it's like doing the things your heart desires.

You wish to own a coffee shop. You find the perfect place in the perfect location. You get the coffee shop. Now what? What impact does it have on others, how would it impact on your daily life? See yourself living the life of owning the coffee shop after you have attained your desire. See your launch party. See your coffee shop getting more busy and popular as each day goes by. See the events and functions taking place over the years developing a successful business and lots of fond memories.

Keep the thoughts flowing and keep building. There's magic in Believing. It all starts with a dream.

The energy of the mind is the essence of life.
Aristotle

Everything around you carries energy. Being positive brings positive outcomes.

Don't forget to tell yourself positive things daily! You must love yourself internally to glow externally.
Hannah Bronfman

Have confidence in your self. Believe your dreams will come true. Have faith in your self. Trust the process. Do the work required, remain focused and committed to what you want or desire. Let your passions be the drive to manifest your desires.

12 SELF ESTEEM

To believe in your dreams, you have to believe in your self.

What lies behind us and what lies before us are tiny matters compared to what lies within us.
Ralph Waldo Emerson

What sets your heart on fire? What are you really good at? What do you love doing?

Every moment in every day you have the opportunity to create your reality. When you have a healthy self-esteem you feel good about yourself, attract the right people and experiences into your life. Your self-esteem affects the quality and success you have in your life. The level of happiness achieved raises your confidence making it easier to cope with life and all its challenges.

Your happiness is your birthright. Believing you are worthy of the very best opens you up to receive all the Universal blessings available to you. Love your self. Stand up for you. We all need to feel loved, valued, appreciated, worthy and significant.

Dare to be different. Say yes to your life, your dreams, your potential. Have the conversation with the one that is holding you back, a family member, spouse, boss so you can clear the air. Their understanding brings blessings to you in the best possible way.

Always make choices and decisions that are best for you. Be discerning and learn to say no when conditions aren't right for you. Be strong. Stand in the power of who you are and what you need and want. When you act in your Highest good you maintain your power and this lifts your self-esteem.

Be confident in the knowing you can handle anything life throws at you. Believe you can create anything you want. You are the leader of your own life. If you don't like something change it. You have the power of choice. Never settle for anything less than what you deserve. How and with whom you spend your life is your choice. Value your happiness. Be strong and stand up for what you want and believe in.

Be mindful of the conversation you have with your self. Do you lift your self up or do you break your self down? Suffering from low self-esteem not only causes confusion, feelings of inertia, cultivates doubt preventing you from reaching your fullest potential. Not believing in yourself you talk your self out of your greatness, your hopes, your dreams, your aspirations thereby preventing you from acting on or pursuing your goals.

Get out of your comfort zone. No matter what circumstances you may find yourself in, you have greatness in you. You have the power to be what you've only dreamed of.

Never let the opinions of others create your reality. Dust your dreams off, it's time for a breakthrough. You get out of life what you put in. Focus on your strengths, work on your weaknesses, do what you love to do.

You are a spiritual being having a human experience. You deserve the very best life has to offer. Be bold, be hungry in your pursuits. Have the courage of your convictions, go after your dreams with passion. Be willing to face life head-on.

Standing up for you and what you believe takes strength and courage. At times you may feel like you don't fit in as a result of your beliefs, leaving you frustrated as no one seems to get you. This can alienate you causing more confusion. All because you are standing up for your-self, and going against what others are saying or doing.

The truth is that our finest moments are most likely to occur when we are feeling deeply uncomfortable, unhappy or unfulfilled. For it is only in such moments, propelled by our discomfort, that we are likely to step out of our ruts and start searching for different ways or truer answers
M Scott Peck

Stand firm. Your commitment, courage, and strength will be tested.

Believing in your self is all that it is required of you. Your values, principles, morals and goals are worth fighting for, even in the face of resistance. Being assertive will help build your confidence and raise your self-esteem.

Stand up for what you believe in. If you can see it you can believe it! Do not be afraid to speak your truths. Be strong. This will lift your self-esteem.

To increase your sense of self-worth, get to know you so you can learn how to be more true to you. Love your self. Accept all of who you are. Let go self-criticism, judgment. Respect you.

Every time you stand up for what you believe in, you get to know you better. Your confidence grows raising your self-esteem. This is how you become wiser, mature and grow. Being wise and trusting yourself more allows you to be more independent, not allowing others opinions to easily influence you anymore. This is how you maintain your sense of self-worth and high self-esteem.

You are the most valuable thing you have in life. How you feel about your self really matters. This forms the basis of your self-esteem and your confidence level. Why it's so important to love and be true to you.

Stand firm in your beliefs, never give up even when others can't see what you can see or share your excitement. The time will come, and you will be grateful you stood up for your self. You will be so pleased only increasing your sense of self and who you truly are, affirming what you really want.

The stronger you feel, the more you lift your self-esteem, the more confident and powerful you'll feel. Feeling strong and confident will make you happy, and you'll feel secure in the knowing you can trust yourself.

Never doubt your self, let your self down or forget about your dreams to garner the approval of others. You deserve to be happy. You know more than anyone else what's best for you. Deep down in your soul you know. Listen. Let your subconscious be your guide.

When you recover or discover something that nourishes your soul and brings joy, care enough about yourself to make room for it in your life."
Jean Shinoda Bolen

Trust what you feel and believe in. This is how you learn about your self. This is how you raise your self-esteem.

Most of the important things in the world have been accomplished by people who had kept on trying when there seemed to be no hope at all.
Dale Carnegie

If you can visualize it, feel it and experience it in your mind, you can have it. When the time is right, you will manifest it. Be patient, trust and believe in you.

Never be afraid to stand up for your self. Life will present you with many situations where it is required of you. See this as a positive experience and opportunity for expansion. Have the courage of your convictions and really trust your self.

You are responsible for the life you lead and the choices you make. To experience happiness and be at peace, always act with integrity and live with a sense of purpose. This is how you grow, become stronger, and the true leader of your own life.

13 HIGHER SELF

Do not follow the ideas of others, but learn to listen to the voice within yourself. Your body and mind will become clear and you will realize the unity of all things.
DOGEN ZENJI : Buddhist monk, philosopher

Transcend your life and all its limitations by connecting with your Higher self.

Step into your light.

You hold all the answers to the questions that you seek.

Listen to your soul. Everything you need to know is within you.

Get out of your head and connect with your heart. Be still. Ask questions of your self. How do you feel? What do you feel? What do you want and where are you going?

When you're in touch with your soul you'll know what your higher purpose on earth is, and you trust your soul knows how to direct your energy towards that purpose.

Trust in your Higher self. Wait for the answers to come. Let your inner voice be your guide. You'll experience a life that is richer and far more rewarding than you ever thought was humanly possible.

If you can't figure out your purpose, figure out your passion. For your passion will lead you right into your purpose.
Bishop TD Jakes

Knowing your true self opens the doors to experiencing life and love with others who match what you want to achieve in life. To experience life and love on this level you get to experience one of the greatest joys one can possibly experience.

By stilling your mind and connecting with your heart, you will create a flow of communication between your conscious mind and your subconscious mind, your Higher self.

Making fewer choices from your mind and spending more time communicating with your heart you'll increase and strengthen the flow between the conscious and the subconscious.

The quieter you become, the more you can hear
Ram Dass

The more you get to know your self, the more you hear. The more you listen, the more aware you become.

The more aware you are, the more easily you hear and find the answers you are looking for.

This is your Higher self guiding you.

You are responsible for your happiness. It is a choice.

Being aware of your thoughts and feelings gives you the option to choose and entertain them or let them go altogether.

You are in control of your emotions. Being in touch with your Higher self helps you embrace and accept all of your emotions instead of fighting or rejecting them.

Accepting your life is in Divine order helps you transmute your experiences and heal as situations change around you.

Love your self. Accept all of who you are. The good and the bad, your strengths and your weaknesses.

We all have a shadow self that co-exists within us. This is where self-sabotaging negative behavior emanates from and only serves to derail or have a massive impact in your life.

When you recognize and accept this part of self can integrate all aspects of your personality to become a whole and true you.

The more you get to know and trust your Higher self the more and more you get the answers that you seek. It's like turning on a light. They call it the "aha" moment of inspiration and enlightenment! The answers you seek will come to you, bringing with it also greater clarity and understanding.

The more aware you become, the more often little insights will come to you. The more insights you get, the more aware you are. The more aware you are, the more confident and the more empowered you will feel.

Making contact with your Higher self develops your senses. Colors appear brighter, your intuition is at an all-time high, and you're able to perceive events before they even unfold.

In touch with your self, life just flows with much more ease. Events occur that benefit you without you even having to ask. You start noticing signs and synchronicities are popping up more and more to help guide you on your path.

Being in touch with your Higher self keeps you vibrating at a higher frequency.

You'll feel good. With all that feel good, positive energy flowing around and through you, you'll keep attracting more of the same back to you.

Everything is in flow and your life can change from positive to negative in an instant as whatever you are feeling is a magnet for your experiences.

Being in touch with your Higher self helps you live a life of truth and integrity making for harmonious relationships and peace full living.

Your home life will improve. Communication opens up thereby improving the relations you have with those you share your life with.

Being in tune with your Higher self means you can make thought full choices and decisions that are in alignment with your truths.

When you live a life of truth your conscious is clear and everything always turns out for the best for all involved. Your life moves with much more ease as you carry no feelings of guilt or shame for events gone by.

When you can see the beauty in the lessons you'll find your past no longer has a hold on you. You see "it" for what it is and accept your experiences have brought you to where you are now giving you the freedom to make new choices and move on with your life.

A great way to make contact with your Higher Self is to get away from the noise and into nature. Spending time outdoors brings peace and quiet and some time alone to process your thoughts. It'll renew your soul and offer a fresh perspective on things.

Conversation enriches the understanding, but solitude is the school of the genius.
Gibbons

When faced with an obstacle or challenge ask your Higher self for help. Be patient for your answers to come. With absolute certainty know in your heart that when the time is right, you will receive the guidance that you need. You will find a solution.

Never allow your ego to diminish your ability to listen.
Gary Hopkins

By listening to your self and following your heart, you will also find yourself experiencing a lot of coincidences and more and more in the right place at the right time. Things just seem to click into place.

These are signs from your Creator showing you are loved and supported and exactly where you are meant to be in that moment in time. Knowing you are Divinely guided will give you the confidence to trust your self more.

Being more in contact with your self gives you a greater understanding of your self, giving you the confidence and courage to be more spontaneous and go with the flow of your life.

When you're happy to go with the flow, your life will move with much more ease versus trying to control your life and find yourself reacting and struggling or having to face obstacles all of the time.

Change and transition isn't always easy. It's normal to feel fear and anxiety. Once you have left what you know and going through the transitional stage of moving into the unknown, you sure to experience a little turbulence along the way.

Be careful not to be caught up in the fear brought on by you or of those around you. Try to stay detached from everything by accepting everything as it is. Separate your self by imagining you're watching your life as if it's a movie. Relax and stay grounded.

You will get through this transitional phase by being calm, letting go and totally trusting the process.

Once you become fearless, life becomes limitless.
Unknown

Trust your self at all times. Go with your feelings. Drop your ego.

When making choices ask yourself if you are making a choice from your heart or is it coming from your ego.

Do what is best for you. Make loving thought full choices.

Choices that are in accordance with your Highest good, as well as for the greater good for all concerned.

Let your sub-conscious guide you rather than trying to figure it out on your own. Ask your Creator for help and trust you will receive it.

Never think too much about a dilemma. Answers come to a relaxed mind; time allows things to fall into place. A calm attitude yields the best results.
Unknown

It takes strength, faith and trust, and the willingness to allow time to go by for things to unfold. You will be guided to the answers that you are looking for. It's a process.

Time does not rush. The right people will come into your life when you need it.

When your soul guides you, it not only gives you direction, it also brings with it a greater understanding of your journey.

Sometimes you find yourself in the middle of nowhere, and sometimes, in the middle of nowhere, you find yourself.
Unknown

Independent and authentic be not afraid to be true to you. You choose if you want to engage in an experience.

When your Higher self is in harmony with your heart, mind and soul you'll be filled with feelings of gratitude for even the smallest of things that comes your way.

Give thanks and be grateful for what they bring.

Communicate with your Higher self all of the time.

Ask for help and trust you will receive it.

Be open to receive so you can take advantage of the opportunities that come up, assisting you to stay on your chosen path.

To the mind that is still, the universe surrenders
Lao Tzu.

Life is to be enjoyed.

When you align with your truth things always turn out for the best for all involved.

Accepting events as they unfold can appreciate the wonder of all that is.

There are infinite possibilities available to you.
Tap into your Higher mind. Listen to it. Let it be your guide.

14 YOUR EGO

Your ego does not define who you are. It simply prevents you from being defined.
Unknown

We all have an ego. Understanding the concept of it will help bring success into your life.

What is your ego?

It's that aspect of self that we call you.

The self-image you have of your self. Who you think and believe you to be.

All your thoughts, all the emotions that you identify with, your beliefs and life's experiences, have come together to create this reality of who you believe you to be.

The ego is strong, constantly judging and criticizing and likes to keep the status quo. It sees itself as separate to every one and every thing.

When things are going well we feel happy and excited, yet when things aren't going so well we feel unhappy and frustrated.

We go through life chasing after things that are good and do everything we can to avoid the things that are bad.

Every time you try to reach for higher consciousness and learning the ego does everything it can to hold you back. It doesn't want you to succeed. It doesn't want you to be become an enlightened and evolved being.

Pay attention to how often you criticize self as well as others. Spend a day monitoring it. You'll gain clarity and increased awareness of how judgmental you really are.

Love is happy when it is able to give something.
The ego is happy when it is able to take something.
Osho

Your Higher self knows everything is relative, we are all connected and form a part of a greater whole. Learning that the ups and downs are a part of life makes it easier to be present in the moment, accepting every day for what it brings.
As your ego dissolves and you see your self as part of a whole you'll notice you're less judgmental, will start moving away from "me" to become "we", and you're more at peace with the authentic and conscious you. You'll find it easier to control your self and less anxious about your future.

Energy flows where attention goes! You have an energetic body. When you make decisions from your ego, you are vibrating on a lower frequency.

Everything else that is vibrating on that same frequency you will draw and attract to you. Whatever you are feeling becomes your point of attraction. Fear, doubt, guilt, shame, jealousy, pride, anger, rejection are all aspects of ego providing negative experiences, keeping you trapped in the cycle of poverty consciousness.

The best way to learn about your self and what triggers you is to pay attention. Every time it happens write it down. What was it that triggered you? How did it make you feel and in return what was your response? You'll start to notice a pattern will emerge.

Being mindful of your experiences helps you to identify these triggers so you can learn to respond to them instead of reacting to them.

You find your self at a point in life where you're happy, things are going well and suddenly "boom" there's a trigger and you're right back to where you came from. Filled with doubt, fear or lacking in motivation.

Life will always present you with situations that grow you.

The challenge lies not in trying to avoid the experiences but to find a healthy balance to keep things calmer. All the obstacles have served a purpose. All the challenges you've gone through have been helping you to become more solid in your future.

When making choices from the ego situations don't turn out as expected. You end up saying and doing things that can have disastrous outcomes and you're not even aware that this is happening to you.

The more subtle triggers are the ones you have to be conscious and aware of as these are the ones you have to watch out for as they have the ability to derail you.

We all have triggers that are unique to us. Identify what it is that makes you fear full. For example you fear not having enough money to meet your needs so you take action that is dishonest and lacking in integrity.

When your reputation is on the line or your beliefs need defending it's a trigger for your lower self. Your ego steps in to protect you.

Dropping your ego is not going to be an easy thing to do. It's like losing a part of who you are. It's part of your personality. This can leave you feeling a little vulnerable as your ego is where you found your strength.

Pay attention to the situations you find your self in. Are you responding or reacting? When you're responding, you've given your response some thought. When you're reacting you haven't given it any thought.

When you respond to life, you are coming from a place of heart. When you react, you are reacting from your ego.

Being mindful takes time and practice. Observing what's happening in your emotional body brings awareness to your situation. Be cautious when reacting as your ego can lash out to protect you if you are feeling vulnerable.

Stop. Check yourself. Walk away if you have to. Make the commitment to never make decisions when you're in ego so you don't do or say something that you may regret later. Do whatever it takes to disengage so you can rid your self of any negative thoughts and words. Look for understanding and calm down. Think about things that make you happy, get you all revved up and excited.

You'll feel your spirits lift raising your frequency to a higher vibration. Once you're vibrating at a higher frequency and you're feeling strong, have given matters much thought and making decisions from your heart, can respond in a way that is constructive and positive for all involved. You'll feel happy and gain peace.

When you find your self in a disagreement with another, ask your self, "Are you coming from a place of love or are you coming from a place of anger?" How important is it to you to find a solution that is best for all concerned or are you acting from your ego, want to win the fight?

You see your ex with a new friend. Are you jealous your ex is happy? Do you feel hurt and angry because you think you've been let down and rejected? Know that all these feelings are aimed at the ego and carrying negative energy.

Whenever in disagreement or when making choices in life, always, always come from the heart, see the good in everyone involved. Have compassion find understanding and a solution that is a win/win outcome for all.

Remember to give what you need. What you put out comes back to you. With compassion and understanding put your self in the others shoes. How would you like it if the other person was reacting to, and treating you the same way you are treating them?

Be humble, accepting and gentle. Learn the art of compromise. When your ego decides to get involved, acknowledge it, then drop it, so you can act in your Highest good.

Ego brings with it lots of anger, conflict, sorrow, shame, guilt, lack of trust and faith.

Your heart will bring you honesty, joy, peace, love and a reason to believe.

When you choose from your heart, you can feel the feeling of that choice. When it sits and feels right you'll find peace. Be humble. Listen to your heart.

When faced with an issue, think about how you are going to respond.

Disengage from the situation so you can come back with a clear head and deal with it in a more empowering way.

Contemplate what would be best for all involved so that everyone comes out a winner. Aim to achieve love and understanding. You can feel when you are making a wrong decision.

If you trust that gut feeling and go with it, you will be guided to making the right choices.

When you come from a place of ego, you are placing too much importance on having power. It could be a simple argument with a friend. Instead of compromising and trying to understand, you go straight in to win. It turns into a game. It doesn't matter what the issue is, so long as you beat the other at the game, at whatever cost you emerge as the winner as you believe this will give you more power.

You think if you have more power you can become a leader. If you are a leader, you will be able to have a great job and make tons of money. If you have a lot of money that will give you a lot more power. If you have a lot more power, you can influence others. The more people you can influence the more you can dominate. If you are dominating everyone, you will feel satisfied with your self.

Nothing could be further from the truth. By feeding your ego, you allow it to affect your life and control you. You'll forget what's really important and how to enjoy being present in the now.

We've emerged from an era where your achievements were based on your material success. The house you live in, the car you drive, how much money you can generate. Success was often gained from taking from others, manipulating them or acting shrewdly. Your success was judged according to what you earned.

Things have changed. Using the same tactics used before will no longer work. It's only when you make choices from your heart that you will succeed.

Going after success purely for monetary gains will no longer support you. Being passionate about what you do and developing that into your career will sustain you.

Be kind and care for those who work with you. By doing what you love, you are generating a lot of feel good energy into your projects which will make them successful, and this will bring abundance. By being a hard-working, action orientated, honest, humble, focusing on what you love not how much money you will earn, you will find abundance physically, materially and spiritually, not just materially.

When going through a tough time financially, if you allow your ego to be affected it will feel like you are losing your sense of personal power. This will bring much anxiety and really make you feel useless, unable, despondent and depressed. So much power has been placed on money that you think it defines who you are.

The lesson is to teach you that you are the power. Everything you need to know is within. You hold all the answers.

Everything in life has its cycles. There will be times of abundance, and you'll experience leaner times. By not handing all your power over to your money when going through leaner times you'll cope better and the "lack of" won't affect you the same way that it used to.

The lesson is to teach you to be self-sufficient and independent.

By finding your inner strength, by not allowing the cycles of flow to get you down, you will no longer be controlled by your wallet, your ego.
It is not how much money you carry in your wallet that defines success. Success is defined by your happiness, the people that love you and the person you have become.

When you use your wealth and your growing empire to feed your ego to gain power over another and do what you have to do to get there, without giving much thought about the consequences of your actions, you are drawing in and putting out negative energy.

Know that whatever actions you take or do you are ultimately doing to self. Every single thing you do, it will get returned to you, "the boomerang effect".

You could find yourself getting involved with another who ends up doing the same to you, or you could end up suffering financial losses. No matter how things unfold, it will result in the sense of loss, leading you to believe you have lost your power.

When living a life of ego, you'll find yourself going through experiences to teach you lessons and humble you. When you believe money buys happiness and makes the world go around, you may find yourself in a situation where it's being taken away from you so that all you're left with is you.

As negative or as painful the experiences may be, there's always a positive in every situation. The good thing that can come from all of this is you will find your self again to remember what truly matters to you.

You ask your Self.
Who am I?
What am I?
Where am I going?

When you get knocked down and have to rebuild your life it's an opportunity to find out who you truly are. By finding self, you will find out what's important to you and what really matters. Through this, you will know who you really are.

Ask your self "What excites me? What are my passions? What do I want to do? By finding self, it will lift your self-esteem and in turn, give you confidence. This will lead to inner strength. Being strong means, you have courage. Having courage is power. When you find your inner power, you live your life according to your truths. You may find you experience some conflict with others, however, once you have decided to follow your heart and live by your truths you will have the strength and courage needed to stand up for your self and not allow others to influence and control you.

When you are standing up for your self and your beliefs, know you are getting there, making progress and it means you are moving away from depending on others and becoming a self-directed conscious soul ready to take responsibility for your self.

Challenging authority figures in your life is a necessary step in your personal growth. Understand too that not everyone and everything is necessarily working against you. Ask the universe for the courage to challenge what oppresses you, and for the wisdom to know when to respect authority. Stand up for what is important to you, and ask for what matters to you. Don't just fight for the sake of fighting or to simply blow off steam. Respect the leadership and rights of others.
Sonia Choquette

Living a humble life focusing on what really makes you happy, you get to appreciate your life by understanding and living with what's really important to you.

What really matters to you? What brings you joy?

Spending time outdoors, the joy of quality time spent with family and friends, all the wonderful experiences each day brings you, the gifts you receive. When you're living a life that makes you happy, you learn how to make choices from your heart.

Happiness blooms in the presence of self-respect and the absence of ego. Love yourself. Love everyone around you. Love everyone in the whole world. Know that your own life is of infinite importance, as is every other life.
Jonathan Lockwood Huie.

At times of recession look around you. There's a lack of money. Lack of money means less power, ego. By dropping the ego, by experiencing lack of, you can come to appreciate both sides of the spectrum and find and truly embrace "who you are, what you are, what you want and where you are going. This is both positive and exciting.

The beauty of a recession is it affects everyone. Those with more have more to lose. Those with less, have less to lose. What it does do, is reduce all of us to the same level. No one is more or less important. We are all the same. We are all affected.
Working in groups is so much more powerful than working on your own. Together we can work on global issues that are important and can create change. Change for the better and the greater good for all.

Be impeccable. Be impeccable with your thoughts, your feelings, and your words.

Love and integrate your ego, your shadow. Love all of self and make choices that come from your heart.

Love everything about you. All the joys, disappointments you've put your self through. All of you. Nobody is perfect. We all have faults. Know this and accept this. By accepting this, you can accept and love all of your self. By loving and accepting every aspect of your self, you won't feel the need to be validated by others. You will feel whole.

There is purpose behind every action, every experience. As you go through challenges you learn grow and become the wiser. As you learn and take steps it's not expected of you to get it right the first time. Nothing happens overnight. Practice makes perfect!

The more you practice the more comfortable and confident you'll become. You'll have good days and you'll have bad days. The more you practice the concept of changing your thinking the more it will become natural for you.

Your happiness matters. Ask your self "what are the triggers that send me into my lower ego self". Making it a daily practice will make you consciously aware of them. It will get easier and easier as time goes by. Make a list so you know what they are, can remedy and heal them by getting to the root of the problem. What created the trigger to start with? Is there past trauma that needs attention and healing? Once you know what the problem is can get the help that you need, can live a conscious and happy life.

You are the leader of your own life. You have the power to manifest the life you wish for. It takes time and practice to see things from a different perspective. When you're no longer willing to continue in the old negative energy that leaves you feeling rejected you're making progress by creating something new for a brighter future.

14.1 FEAR

You can conquer almost any fear if you will only make up your mind to do so. For remember, fear doesn't exist anywhere except in the mind.
Dale Carnegie

You can live a life of fear or you can live the life of your dreams. This is a choice and only you can make it.

Assess your life. Everything you have been going through is a result of your choices. Are you satisfied with the decisions you have made? Are you happy and doing what you love or do you want and believe at the core of your being that there is something better out there for you?

We all have fears, blocks and limitations that hold us back. This is where your growth lies. Go through the process and you'll be rewarded for all your hard work. For on the opposite side of fear lies immense strength.

When you're not living up to your true potential and experiencing the life of your dreams look at fear. Fear of not being good enough. Fear of not being loved, appreciated or respected. Fear of failure. Fear of success. Fear of not having enough. Fear of being alone.

Fear only prevents you from standing in the way of your greatness.

If you fear it, don't want it, just don't think about it. Instead of spending time focusing on what you do want, you spend time worrying about what you don't want. Energy flows where attention goes. By focusing on what you don't want you manifest exactly that because you are feeding it energy.

What fears are you holding onto? What fears are keeping you stuck preventing you from moving forward? What fears are preventing you from living out your true potential? What fears are standing in the way of your happiness?

Acknowledge and embrace your fears and let go. Drop your thoughts and move on. Fear loses its power when it's not getting any attention.

Having fears is normal, but once you're willing to face them will find the fear of was greater than the actual fear itself.

Yesterday is gone, tomorrow hasn't happened. All we have is the present. Worrying about your future only breeds fear. Fear of the unknown. When you present in the moment you'll find your life is on track and no matter what life throws at you, you manage with ease.

Trust and believe in your self. You have to take that first step toward going after what you want. Show self-respect by always showing up, and with intention and focus give it all you've got. And if you should fail you try and try and try again. Because it's better to try and fail than to never try at all. You'll only be left wondering what could have, would have happened had you tried.

No matter what challenges or difficulties you may face you are strong enough to handle them. You're Divinely guided. Will never be given anything you cannot cope with. The support will always be there, you only have to ask for it.

Challenges are never easy but that's what you have to go through to get where you want to be. There are lessons to be learned, experiences to be had, growth to be made. All you have to do is commit to the journey, take a step, have fun and enjoy the ride.

Constantly monitor your thoughts and always be aware of your feelings. As your thoughts affect your feelings and your feelings are your point of attraction whatever you fear, you are creating.

Build yourself up by being your greatest supporter. Speak to you as if you were your best friend! Should you find you beating your self up with self-criticism or judgment let it go. Drop it. Be patient, loving and kind. Use your energy to uplift, inspire and motivate you in the same manner you would an other. Gently nudge your self to do what you have to do to keep moving forward.

What do you fear? What is standing in the way of your progress?

We all have fears, blocks and limitations that hold us back. This is where your growth lies. Go through the process and you'll be rewarded for all your hard work. When you not living up to your true potential and experiencing the life of your dreams, know it is fear that is holding you back.

Let your fear of, be the motivator to propel you forward.

Be conscious of your fears. Be careful about what you are thinking about and focusing all your energy on, the little or big things making you nervous, scared or completely immobilizing you. Stop. By giving your thoughts and fears energy, you are feeding and creating those thoughts ready to start turning them into your reality.

Pay attention. Constantly monitor your thoughts. By focusing on the things that you fear you are feeding that fear with a lot of energy.

For example, you start off with a simple fear of not passing your exams. You are running out of time, there is so much work to do, and you are afraid you will not be ready to write when the time arrives. You go over it again and again, day after day, this just making you stress out more, you can't see how you will be ready and start entertaining how that will then impact on your life.

If you don't pass your exams, you will not be able to join your friends on the holiday that's been arranged as a celebration of your success. You're thinking about all the things you will miss out on and how sad that would be for you.

The time to write arrives, you've been stressing so much about failing you're simply not ready and confident enough to write the exam and guess what, you don't qualify. You are mad at yourself, you blame others for your set back, you're angry at life and miss the time with your friends. You really feel very down and sorry for yourself. One thing happens after another. Things just go from bad to worse.

The minute you worry about something or find yourself dwelling on a certain fear, drop it, fast. Rather ask for help to solve your dilemma and let it go. Quickly find something positive or happy to think about. Know and affirm you will find a solution to your problem, and just keep your mind off whatever is bothering you.

By giving fear energy, you are drawing in and attracting everything else that is vibrating on the same frequency as that fear. Like a magnet. Soon you will have a load of other things in your life to worry and fear about, not just the initial concern that you started with.

All this was born from one simple thought, action or word.

Do something positive. Go out there, do some good deeds, help someone, be kind to someone.

Volunteer your services to the Community in whatever way you feel fit, be it your time, physically, spiritually or materially.

Giving of self and helping others, will not only make you feel good, which will help you maintain a positive attitude, it will also be sending a whole lot of good energy back to you.

Trust and be conscious of information that pops into your mind, as well as note the people who come into your life and listen to what they have to say, as their words or kind gestures will offer solutions, help you, support you.

Stay in the moment and deal with each little situation as it comes up. You will know what needs your attention and when.

Timing is just as much an important ingredient.

When the time is right, you'll easily reach successful outcomes. The outcome that you desire as well as positive for all involved.

Sometimes what you want and when you want it is not in line with the timing of the want. Sometimes you have to wait for things to unfold around you before your desire can become a reality. And by not always knowing what's going on "behind the scenes" your faith will be tested.

Trust all is well, and then when the time is right it will come to you for your attention.

There are great creativity and progress in the act of waiting. If you are experiencing delays and frustrations so that it seems your goals will never be realized, do not become resigned and give up. Gently let go of the resistance that waiting often creates, and cultivate a patient certainty that the door of opportunity will appear by and by. This inner act will work the magic. While you labor and wait, remember, to have fun.
Claire Nahmad

Stand up for your self.

Trust you can handle any situation you may find yourself in.

Believe.

The less you fear, the less you will find to fear, the more your confidence will improve, the more you will learn about your self, the more your self-esteem will grow, the stronger you become.

Life will become more exciting and enjoyable which is much better than spending your time fearing what "might or might not be" and hiding away from the world.

When you stand in the greatness of who you are, fear of will simply dissipate.

14.2 POVERTY CONSCIOUSNESS

Poverty is not an accident. Like slavery and apartheid, it is man-made and can be removed by the actions of human beings
Nelson Mandela

Poverty consciousness is ego based beliefs, feelings, thoughts, values and attitudes. When you're in poverty consciousness you have a fear of lack. You associate your experiences of fear of safety on a deeper level meaning fear of not having enough. Fear of lack of money, fear of not having enough material objects that will enable your security.

When feeling threatened or vulnerable you know you're in poverty conscious as you don't believe you'll have what you need to feel safe, secure and supported.

Consumed by fear of survival and threats of poverty keeps you trapped in a never ending cycle of poverty consciousness.

When you accept poverty consciousness as a way of life you become a puppet to life. You simply go on living, barely surviving, day after day, caught up in a cycle of poverty that never ends.

Constantly feeling insecure can trigger feelings of hopelessness and despair having a negative impact on your self-esteem and confidence.

You believe you'll find security from all the material objects you surround yourself with to manage the unconscious fears that are a result of feeling totally helpless when facing threats.

If chasing success is what motivates you, you won't be able to sustain your self. It's a successful mind and passionate heart that keeps prosperity flowing.

Becoming obsessed with material objects as a means to validate your security and increase feelings of self-worth, or as a means to distract one from facing ones feelings or challenging issues can leave one feeling empty, spiritually disconnected.

Filling your life with material objects won't satisfy your spiritual needs or bring you that feeling of wholeness you so deeply desire.

It's the fear of not having enough that motivates one to take action and go out to buy more things believing they will help you feel better and offer more security.

Poverty consciousness fears are ingrained deep within your subconscious mind. All it takes is a trigger to get them to surface into the conscious mind as fear based thoughts and feelings.

Giving these fear based thoughts and feelings attention creates a flow of negative energy. The more energy you give them the greater the energetic flow thereby increasing the fears borne out of poverty consciousness.

When you're in poverty consciousness you believe if you not abundant with material goods you are considered to be unsuccessful and worthless.

Being in poverty consciousness is not measured by how much money or success you have. Many have an abundance of material assets yet they feel a deep desire to accumulate more. It is never enough.

When I chased after money, I never had enough. When I got my life on purpose and focused on giving of myself and everything that arrived into my life, then I was prosperous. Wayne Dyer

Poverty consciousness is a fear based state of being where you're lacking in spiritual beliefs. It is an ego based, limited mindset of fear of lack that has led to high levels of poverty plaguing the masses of humanity, increasing the levels of greed and corruption we are constantly witnessing around the globe.

Abundance is your birthright. We are all equally free to flourish.

Transmuting poverty consciousness into prosperity consciousness is a critical step in paving the way for a future that is peace full, brighter and abundant for all.

Pay attention to the energy you are putting out, how you feel, your thoughts and your words.

By constantly worrying and repeating the words poor, worry, loss, you are creating and attracting situations that draw that to you, and in return live a life with poor, worry and loss as your reality.

When you worry you don't have enough money, you're giving it so much attention you will soon have many reasons to worry about not having enough money and so the cycle continues, you're constantly given many more reasons to worry about not having enough money.

By worrying about something, we are giving it attention, feeding it energy turning a small issue into a big concern. That worry attracts more worry.

It's the middle of the month, you already out of funds, you're stressing out as you don't know how you are going to get through the month and then to top it your car breaks down. Not knowing how you are going to pay for the repairs, you stress some more, and your washing machine also goes on the blink! That gets you going, now its living expenses, car and washing issues. How are you going to get your laundry done? You'll need funds and a car to get to the closest Laundromat. The thought of all of this weighs you down. Not long after that your television set pops. You stress, and stress and more and more all sorts of little things around you are going wrong, and you hear yourself say "I just can't believe it, it's not fair, everything that can go wrong is going wrong". You don't have enough funds to get through the month as it is, and now all these added expenses have added strain and anxiety when you're already stressed out because you can't meet your needs financially. You really now do have no money and lots of worry to worry about!

By saying "I can't afford it", you won't be able to afford it. Everything you feel, say or think has an impact in your life as that creates your reality.

Whatever is going on in your inner world is reflected back at you in your outer world.

Think big, pretend, imagine, feel, do whatever you have to do to be it.

When faced with insurmountable challenges let go and believe with utmost faith the answers, solutions and support will come. Stay present in the now, ask for help then act like you already have it!

Impossible is just a big word thrown around by small men who find it easier to live in the world they've been given than to explore the power they have to change it. Impossible is not a fact. It's an opinion. Impossible is not a declaration. It's a dare. Impossible is potential. Impossible is temporary. Impossible is Nothing.
Powered by: Adidas

You are a product of your thoughts. By denying your self, by holding back, you are ultimately preventing your self from enjoying yourself, preventing anything from coming in and will remain in that negative thought pattern until you change it.

Pretend.
Fake it till you make it!

Act like you have all you need and can attain anything you would like at any given time. You go shopping, and you see something you would love, but would normally sigh and affirm you cannot afford it, so with sadness walk off. Change that. When you see it, pretend you can have it. Affirm "I'll take that", and with expectant joy and excitement walk off. Always pretend to be living the life in the now that you are aspiring to. Act like "it is".

Happiness is your birth right. Obtaining wealth and financial freedom is an important part of your spiritual journey. Own your right to happiness. Honor your self by committing to the process and following through with action. All that is asked of you is to practice self-love, live the life you love and have fun. Move toward a future that you want and enjoy. Being happy is the key to your success.

To find peace be prepared to face your truths. Dig deep. The deeper you go, the more you uncover. The more you're able to uncover, the more you're able to bring about changes in practical ways to help you to feel more grounded and secure.

Be honest about where you are in life, why you are where you are, how you feel about it and what you want and love.

When you're ready to be honest with self can take action in support of that truth as now you understand it! With clarity can move in a direction of greater love for self by applying it in ways that help you to live a better life by being clear about what it is that you need to be at peace with your self.

You are responsible for the life you lead. Honor your truths and sense of self. Make choices that are best for you as well as all involved.

Connecting with your inner self you'll learn to trust your self more.

Be the driver of your own life. Take the lead and move in the direction that inspires and excites you.

Focus on what you want. Set clear intentions, draw up a plan and take action. Make moves toward your dreams.

What you put out you get back. Hard work, focus and commitment bring their own rewards.

Don't endure life, enjoy life! Approach it with a greater sense of belief that great things and opportunities can and do happen.

It is that belief that will drive the conversations and synchronistic moments that can make it so.

Live a life of purpose. Do something you love.

Use the skills, creativity and knowledge you've been blessed with to bring about the change you want.

Find a way to heal childhood trauma's and subconscious thoughts.

Change your attitude and ideas about wealth and money.

The people you come into contact with are drawn and attracted to you by whatever energy or information you are putting out there. Show your gratitude.

Be organized, have a plan, get a system going, do whatever you need to do to set yourself up so when others approach you're prepared and ready.

At times of recession we are all affected. Those with more have more to lose. Those with less, have less to lose. What it does do, is reduce all of us to the same level.

No one is more or less important.

We are all the same. We are all affected.

Money is the currency used for the purchase of experiences and things. To have one we give another.

It is an equal exchange of energy.

Through entrepreneurship we can all share our gifts, support one another and build our wealth.
Working in groups is so much more powerful than working on your own.

Together we can work on global issues that are important and can create change.

Change for the better and the greater good for all.

Be thankful for what you have and generous with what you share.

Turn your desire to have more into a yearning to give more, do more, and be more for others.

All that you are and all that you do will always come back to appreciate you.

15 GIFT OF GIVING

We make a living by what we get. We make a life by what we give.
Winston S. Churchill

The essence of generosity is when your mind can let go of attachment, the need to cling onto others or perform acts of selfishness. When you give, give with an open heart and without any expectation to receive anything in return.

Giving of your self will make a better person out of you. When we give to impress others or for the sake of looking good, the intention behind the giving is not pure, it has your own self-interest at heart. Being selfish comes from your ego keeping you vibrating on a lower frequency whereas generosity and kindness vibrate at a very high frequency.

When you nurture your self as well as others you are creating beautiful surroundings opening you up to beautiful circumstances.

There's nothing more fulfilling than experiencing how giving of your self has enabled an other. All that feel good, grateful energy that the other feels is directed right back at you, filling you up with feel good energy in return.

With action comes reaction. You have to give in order to get.

When we no longer feel greed for things, we can become passionate about meeting the needs of others with what we have. Being generous with your time, resources or possessions will be worth so much more than what you give up.

Being generous isn't something that comes naturally.

It means being helpful and assisting others in a way that brings positive results, contributing towards their wellbeing. It is only through the mere act of giving that we get to know and experience the joy of the action.

When you carry out a helpful act you give to the other thereby influencing them in a positive way bringing about satisfactory results. Being help full means being generous with your time. Care for others. Allow your self to feel love and affection towards them.

By being kind and generous, showering others with gifts or the gift of your time, you are actually giving back to your self.

Remember that the happiest people are not those getting more, but those giving more.
H. Jackson Brown Jr.

Being humble means putting others needs before your own. Be kind towards others. Life is about what you can give, not about what you can get.

It's not how much you do but how much love you put into the doing that matters.
Mother Teresa

You'll find it very nourishing to be more generous with your self. By giving of your self, it nourishes you to see how much it has helped the other person, which in turn will make you feel good.

Humility does not mean you think less of yourself, it means you think of yourself less
Ken Blanchard

Every single thing you do it will get returned to you. The very act of giving opens you up to receive. When you need a shoulder to cry on, a friend is there, when you need help, help is there, when you need support, support is there.

It is one of the most beautiful compensations of this life that no man can sincerely try to help another without helping himself.
Ralph Waldo Emerson

We aren't always able to give monetary gifts, so these little gestures from your heart are even better as they carry with them the gift of love. You'll feel great for being able to give of your self, make a difference in someone's life and enjoy feeling loved in return.

Give items you no longer use or need to someone who will. Clear out and tidy your closets. By having an order in your cupboards, you'll bring order into your life. By removing unwanted items from your cupboard and giving those unwanted items to another who will, it will not only give them much joy; it also creates space in your cupboard for new things to come into your life. This is creating a flow of new energy around you.

We must give more in order to get more. It is the generous giving of ourselves that produces the generous harvest.
Orison Swett Marden

The Universe is constantly sending you gifts too, however we are not always able to see or recognize them. When one is so busy thinking and worrying about what you don't have, you'll fail to see the opportunities, the gifts that you do have.

You are amped to see the latest movie everyone is raving about. You have plans to go with your friends, and this is making you very excited. The big day arrives but it's raining, you have no car, your day is cancelled. This saddens you. You're sitting thinking about all the things you were going to do with your friends that day, and you're angry, disappointed and upset that you're at home instead.

The phone rings. It's a friend you have not seen in years. He's only here for a few hours would it be possible for him to pick you up and the two of you spend the afternoon together. Wow, how lucky you are that you have no plans and are available to spend the time with your friend.

Remember something positive always comes from a negative situation, you only have to see it. Although you wanted to do what you wanted to, and are disappointed events did not unfold the way you thought you wanted them to, by accepting the situation for what it is it leaves you feeling grateful and appreciative of what did come from the situation instead. Things always happen for a reason. Be happy with what you have whilst working toward what you want.

So much has been given to me, I have not the time to ponder over that which has been denied.
Helen Keller

Before you start your day give thanks for the gifts you received the day before and ask what gifts are in store for you today. Be open to receiving them. With gratitude count your blessings. List your experiences, things you received or the opportunities given. Time with friends, chocolate, beautiful weather, a warm bed, a loving family, fun with your partner, a wonderful meal, new shoes, time for self, take note of everything you receive and have, and be grateful for them.

The more grateful you are the more things you will be given to be grateful about. You'll start noticing more and more how many gifts and wonderful blessings you do have in your life. Opportunities are always around. You only have to open your eyes to see them.

You'll start appreciating more and more what you do have and spend less time thinking about what you wish you had.

The joy of giving does not come with expectation of what you're going to get in return. Give because you want to give and not because you want something. When you give to get it changes the intention of the action, all you're going to get is feeling like you're a victim or being taken advantage of.

Give of your self because you have the desire to give. Be generous with your time, your love, your heart and your resources. Connecting with an other is where the true gift lies.

You can be generous with your time and resources whilst at the same time set healthy boundaries or learn to say no. Only give of your self or agree to things you are willing to do so that the energy behind the action is filled with joy instead of saying yes because you want something in return albeit gratitude for your efforts or appreciation for your generosity. You want to say yes because you really want to help. Once you agree to help, be passionate about what you're doing otherwise don't do it at all. Should you be asked to help and you don't have the time or resources, simply say so. Be honest.

It is true when you focus more on what you can give versus what you can get you will be happier and more successful, however you have to always come from a place of love, generosity and desire to express your love and service to an other with no attachment to the outcome or expectations of getting things in return.

Compassion is key. Start by being compassionate toward self. When you're compassionate toward self you become aware and kind towards others. With kindness comes truth. One cannot fake kindness. It's real and the other feels it deep down at the core of their being. Nothing beats that exhilarating feeling you get in return when you feel the response to the others joy.

The secret to be found in wealth and abundance lies in the very act of giving and feeling complete. Be generous with others. You can never give too much when you're giving with an open heart.

The universe loves a giving heart. The more you give, the more will be given to you to give. It is a constant flow of positive energy growing in momentum around you. Helping others opens doors to helping your self. It is the equal exchange of energy. By giving of your self you are expressing who you really are as kindness motivates the truth.

Being wonderful, being glorious, your authentic self allows you to see every moment as an opportunity to recreate your self and start anew. As you recreate your self to the highest vision of who you really are, and if you practice doing this every day your whole life will fall into place and make sense to you.

You get to experience a life that is authentic to you in a way that makes sense to the world and that's how life changes and becomes the miracle it was meant to be. The moment you decide to be what your soul always intended for you to be.

It is love and wisdom that goes around and continues to move us forward on our spiritual evolution.

And let it be.

Daisy Flower – Meaning, Symbolism and Colors
By Flower Meanings

The message behind the daisy flower is the message of purity and hope. This gorgeous and gentle flower is a perfect gift for someone who needs a little bit of support and a ray of sunshine in their life.

Daisy flowers are perfect symbols of innocence and positive energy. It is a symbol of a new beginning and it is a perfect gift for someone who is on the verge of a breakthrough in his life and is ready to make a big step towards the future. Daisy flowers represent a new dawn and start of something amazing and new. They close their petals each night and open them up every morning, which can also be a symbol for a new beginning in life. Giving Daisies to someone who is making a big step forward is the best way to use this symbolic meaning.

In addition to all of the above, in this flower, the strongest image is the persistence, perseverance and unobtrusive power. Daisy, just like the person you give to this flower, appreciates simplicity and modesty, but also counts on your loyalty and patience.

https://flowermeanings.org/daisy-flower-meaning/

Wishing you love, light and many blessings as you embark on the journey of self discovery.

May your soul find its way home.

Printed in Great Britain
by Amazon